Go, little book, and wish to all
Flowers in the garden, meat in the hall,
A bin of wine, a spice of wit,
A house with lawns enclosing it,
A living river by the door
A nightingale in the sycamore.

—ROBERT LOUIS STEVENSON

Next to doing things that deserve to be written, there is nothing that gets a man more credit, or gives him more pleasure, than to write things that deserve to be read.

— LORD CHESTERFIELD
Letters to His Son, 1739.

Mark Twain

The New

Joy

of

Words

*Selections of literature
expressing beauty, history, humor, inspiration
or wisdom . . .
which are a joy to read
and read again*

J. G. FERGUSON PUBLISHING COMPANY
CHICAGO

For Pat Happy Birthday May 3, 1969

[handwritten signature]

MANY TIMES the physical form or appearance of a poem, quotation or story influences the impulse to read it. Too frequently, great words in the world of literature become buried in the archives of libraries or bibliophiles because they are sandwiched into pages of small print on yellowed paper, musty with age and dusty with disuse. Most great writing is undated as to time, era or circumstance. It is just as fresh and compelling now as it was the year of its creation. Emily Dickinson passed away in 1885, yet her thoughts as expressed in poetry have the same soft lilt and poignancy today as they had in 1890, when they were published. The same holds true for most of the statesmen, philosophers, essayists and storytellers, whose works are included in this selection.

To uncover a few of the gems from the literary past along with some contemporary items of wit, wisdom or humor, and to present them in a manner that will attract by typographic originality, appealing design, and unusual arrangement, have been the guiding objectives in this creation. To give pleasure by a renewal of old literary acquaintances, and by an introduction to a few old and new authors whom you may have missed in your reading up to now, is another prime purpose of this miscellany. He, who does not derive a vicarious thrill in recognizing a passage of poetry or sterling prose, is indeed most unusual or perhaps so wonderfully versed, any selection made for him by some other editor would fall far short of his tastes. This is very understandable, so we have made no effort by plan or outline to "educate." Our mission is to amuse and inspire. Yet, it is our belief that some slight self-improvement must follow as a natural course of reading the words of the sages of the ages. Cicero said it so much better than we can:

> "Other relaxations are peculiar to certain
> times, places, and stages of life, but the study
> of letters is the nourishment of our youth and
> the joy of our old age. They throw an addi-
> tional splendor on prosperity, and are the re-
> sources and consolation of adversity; they
> delight at home, and are no embarrassment

abroad; in short, they are company to us at night, our fellow travellers on a journey, and attendants at our rural recesses."

We are indebted to many authors and publishers whose works have been included. Likewise, we gratefully acknowledge the work of the artists of the Brown and Bigelow Company, particularly Ken Haag, who painted the subjects appearing in color-process. As always, the Creative, Sales Promotion and Purchasing Departments of the same company have been instrumental in whatever excellence this volume can claim.

In the preparation of this edition of The NEW JOY OF WORDS we are indebted for purposes of reference or actual usage to the following books, authors and publishers: Stevenson's Book of Quotations, by Burton Stevenson, Cassell and Co., Ltd., London, Toronto; Poems by Emily Dickinson, Roberts Bros., Boston; Lincoln and other Poems, Edwin Markham, The McClure Company, N.Y.; Surf and Wave: The Sea as sung by the Poets, by Anna T. Ward, Thomas Y. Crowell & Co.; Lyrics for Freedom, Carleton, N. Y.; Ten Thousand Wonderful Things, by E. F. King, George Routledge and Sons, London; Lyrics of the XIXth Century, Chas. Scribner's Sons, N. Y.; A Book of Heroic Verse, by Arthur Burrell, E. P. Dutton & Co.; What Makes A Friend, by Volney Streamer, Brentano's; The Complete Poetical Works of Edgar Allen Poe, by James A. Harrison, Thomas Y. Crowell Co., N. Y.; The Lore of the Wanderer, an open-air anthology by George Goodchild, E. P. Dutton and Co.; Poet's Wit and Humour, by W. H. Wills, Joseph Cundall, London; Familiar Short Sayings of Great Men, by Samuel A. Bent, Chatto and Windus, London; The Lark, by Bruce Porter and Gelett Burgess, Wm. Dorpy, San Francisco; Weather Proverbs, by H. H. C. Dunwoody, Government Printing Office; Tennyson's Poetical Works, Houghton Mifflin & Co., Boston, N. Y.; The Spell of the Yukon and Other Verses, by Robert W. Service, Barse and Hopkins, N. Y.; A Library of Poetry and Song by William Cullen Bryant, J. B. Ford & Co., N, Y.; The Poetical Works of Oliver Wendell Holmes, Houghton Mifflin Co.; Shelley's Complete Poetical Works, Houghton Mifflin & Co.; Wine From These

Grapes, by Edna St. Vincent Millay, Harper and Brothers, New York and London; Ailes D'Alouette, by F. W. Bourdillon, Roberts Bros., Boston; The Trail of Lewis and Clark, by Olin D. Wheeler, G. P. Putnam's Sons, New York; Southey's Common-Place Book, by John Wood Warter, Harper and Brothers, N. Y.; A Further Range, by Robert Frost, Henry Holt and Co., N. Y.; Wau-Bun, by Mrs. John H. Kinzie, Rand-McNally & Co., Chicago; Bawdy Ballads and Lusty Lyrics, Maxwell Droke, Indianapolis; The Works of Jonathon Swift, Henry G. Bohn, London; A Treasury of Humorous Poetry, by Frederic L. Knowles, Dana Estes and Co., Boston; The Rivers of America, The Illinois, by James Gray, Farrar & Rinehart, N. Y.; Golden Numbers, McClure Phillips & Co., N. Y.; Book of Days, by R. Chambers, W & R Chambers, London; The Speaker's Treasury of Stories for all Occasions, by Herbert V. Prochnow, Prentice-Hall, Inc.; Ancient Gems in Modern Settings, by G. B. Grundy, Albert and Charles Boni, N. Y.; The Statesmanship of Andrew Jackson, by Francis N. Thorpe, The Tandy Thomas Company, N. Y.; Weather Opinions, by Jennie Day Haines, Paul Elder & Co., San Francisco; The Washoe Giant in San Francisco, George Fields, San Francisco; Biographical Memoirs of the Illustrious Gen. George Washington, Joseph Dix, Barnard, Vt.; The Quaint Comedy of Love, Wooing and Mating, E. P. Dutton & Co.; The Complete Poetical Works of Bret Harte, Chatto and Windus, London; In Flanders Fields, by Lt. Col. John McCrae, M.D.; G. P. Putnam's Sons, N. Y.; Recollections and Letters of Gen. Robt. E. Lee, Doubleday Page and Co., N. Y.; An American Anthology, by Edmund Clarence Stedman, Houghton Mifflin and Co., Boston. The poems and prose selected from Smoke and Steel by Carl Sandburg, copyright, 1920, by Harcourt, Brace & World, Inc.; renewed 1948, by Carl Sandburg. Reprinted by permission of the publishers.

—THOMAS C. JONES

TABLE OF CONTENTS

Literature of Interest

TABLE OF CONTENTS

History

TABLE OF CONTENTS

Mostly for Ladies

TABLE OF CONTENTS

Grow Old Along with Me

Mostly for Men

TABLE OF CONTENTS

TABLE OF CONTENTS

The World of Books

TABLE OF CONTENTS

..... OF THINGS THAT ARE
AND OF THINGS THAT ARE TO BE

by

Oliver Wendell Holmes

As I GROW older I grow calm. If I feel what are perhaps an old man's apprehensions, I do not lose my hopes. I do not pin my dreams for the future to my country or even to my race. I think it probable that civilization somehow will last as long as I care to look ahead—perhaps with smaller numbers, but perhaps also bred to greatness and splendor by science. I think it is not improbable that man, like the grub that prepares a chamber for the winged thing it has never seen but is to be—that man may have cosmic destinies that he does not understand. And so beyond the vision of battling races and an impoverished earth I catch a dreaming glimpse of peace.

The other day my dream was pictured to my mind. It was evening. I was walking homeward on Pennsylvania Avenue near the Treasury, and as I looked to the west the city was aflame with scarlet and crimson from the setting sun. But like the note of downfall in Wagner's opera, below the skyline there came from little globes the pallid discord of the electric lights. And I thought to myself the Gotterdammerung will end, and from those globes clustered like evil eggs will come new masters of the sky. It is like the times in which we live. But then I remembered the faith that I partly have expressed, faith in a universe not measured by our fears, a universe that has thought and more than thought inside it, and as I gazed, after the sunset and above the electric lights there shone the stars.

All are but parts of one stupendous whole,
Whose body Nature is, and God the soul.

Essay on Man, Alexander Pope

The Time Is Short!

Every man has two educations—that which is given to him, and the other, that which he gives to himself. Of the two kinds, the latter is by far the most valuable. Indeed all that is most worthy in a man, he must work out and conquer for himself. It is that, that constitutes our real and best nourishment. What we are merely taught, seldom nourishes the mind like that which we teach ourselves.

—RICHTER

A gentleman, in the vulgar, superficial way of understanding the word, is the devil's christian. But to throw aside these polished and too current counterfeits for something valuable and sterling, the real gentleman should be gentle in everything, at least in everything that depends on himself,—in carriage, temper, constructions, aims, desires. He ought therefore to be mild, calm, quiet, even temperate,—not hasty in judgment, not exorbitant in ambition, not overbearing, not proud, not rapacious, not oppressive; for these things are contrary to gentleness. Many such gentlemen are to be found, I trust; and many more would be were the true meaning of the name borne in mind and duly inculcated.

—HARE

You who are letting miserable misunderstandings run on from year to year, meaning to clear them up some day;

You who are keeping wretched quarrels alive because you cannot quite make up your mind that now is the day to sacrifice your pride and kill them;

You who are passing men sullenly upon the street, not speaking to them out of some silly spite, and yet knowing that it would fill you with shame and remorse if you heard that one of those men were dead tomorrow morning;

You who are letting your neighbor starve, till you hear that he is dying of starvation;

Or letting your friend's heart ache for a word of appreciation or sympathy, which you mean to give him someday;

If you only could know and see and feel, all of a sudden, that *"the time is short,"* how it would break the spell! How you would go instantly and do the thing which you might never have another chance to do.

A TASTE FOR READING

GIVE A MAN THIS TASTE
(AND THE MEANS OF GRATIFYING IT)
AND YOU CAN HARDLY FAIL
TO MAKE HIM A HAPPY MAN.
YOU PLACE HIM IN CONTACT
WITH THE BEST SOCIETY
IN EVERY PERIOD OF HISTORY,
WITH THE WISEST AND WITTIEST,
THE TENDEREST AND BRAVEST
WHO HAVE ADORNED HUMANITY.
YOU MAKE HIM
A DENIZEN OF ALL NATIONS,
A CONTEMPORARY OF ALL AGES.

SIR JOHN HERSCHEL, *Address at the opening of Eton Library, 1833*

DEFINITIONS OF "A FRIEND"

The first person who comes in when the whole world has gone out.

A bank of credit on which we can draw supplies of confidence, counsel, sympathy, help and love.

One who combines for you alike the pleasures and benefits of society and solitude.

A jewel whose lustre the strong acids of poverty and misfortune cannot dim.

One who multiplies joys, divides griefs, and whose honesty is inviolable.

A true test of friendship, to sit or walk with a friend for an hour in perfect silence without wearying of one another's company.

INEXPENSIVE CYNICISMS:

A Profit is not without Honor save in Boston.

A Poet is not without Honor save in San Francisco.

A Lark in the Hand gathers no Moss.

Accessions will happen in the best regulated Families.

One touch of Nature makes the whole World blush.

The Course of true Love is the Route of all Evil.

Flirtation is the Thief of Time.

The Milk of human Kindness never did run smooth.

'T is a mean Door that hath no Key Hole.

Poets are born not Maids.

Western communications corrupt good Manners.

Of two Devils choose the Prettier.

It is always the Unexpensive that happens.

If a Man kiss thee on one Cheek, turn to him the Other also. So shines a good Deed in a naughty Girl.

WOMAN'S WILL

That man's a fool who tries by art and skill
To stem the torrent of a woman's will:
For if she will, she will; you may depend on't
And if she won't, she won't—and there's an end on't.

— EIGHTEENTH CENTURY

"Some men are like pyramids"

Happiness is not the end of life: character is.

———

The truest self-respect is not to think of self.

———

Selfishness is that detestable vice which no one will forgive in others, and no one is without in himself.

———

The real man is one who always finds excuses for others, but never for himself.

———

Success is full of promise till men get it; and then it is a last-year's nest, from which the birds have flown.

———

The philosophy of one century is the common-sense of the next.

———

Men are called fools in one age for not knowing what they were called fools for averring in the age before.

———

Not that which men do worthily, but that they do successfully, is what history makes haste to record.

———

Some men are like pyramids, which are very broad where they touch the ground, but grow narrow as they reach the sky.

— HENRY WARD BEECHER
From "Life Thoughts"

I can find no meaning which I can attach to what is termed good, if I take away from it the pleasures obtained by taste, the pleasures which come from listening to music, the charm derived by the eyes from the sight of figures in movement, or other pleasures produced by any of the senses in the whole man. —EPICURUS

EVERY MAN HAS A MISSION
TO HELP HIS FELLOW-BEINGS

Let us do all we can in our day and generation in the cause of humanity. Every man has a mission from God to help his fellow-beings. Though we differ in faith, thank God there is one platform on which we stand united, and that is the platform of charity and benevolence. We cannot, indeed, like our Divine Master, give sight to the blind, hearing to the deaf, speech to the dumb, and strength to the paralyzed limb, but we can work miracles of grace and mercy by relieving the distress of our suffering brethren. And never do we approach nearer to our Heavenly Father than when we alleviate the sorrows of others. Never do we perform an act more Godlike than when we bring sunshine to hearts that are dark and desolate. Never are we more like to God than when we cause the flowers of joy and of gladness to bloom in souls that were dry and barren before. "Religion," says the apostle, "pure and undefiled before God and the Father, is this: To visit the fatherless and widows in their tribulation, and to keep oneself unspotted from the world." Or, to borrow the words of pagan Cicero, *Homines ad deos nulla re propius accedunt quam salutem hominibus dando.* (There is no way by which men can approach nearer to the gods than by contributing to the welfare of their fellow-creatures.)

— CARDINAL GIBBONS

He who does something *at the head of* one *regiment will eclipse him who does* nothing *at the head of a hundred.*
—ABRAHAM LINCOLN, *letter to Gen. Hunter.*

"THOUGHTS"

"Do every act in thy life
as if it were the last"

by Marcus Aurelius

"Be not afraid because some time thou must cease to live, but fear never to have begun truly to live."

_____

"If it is not right, do not do it. If it is not true, do not say it."

_____

"The pride which is proud of its want of pride is the most intolerable pride of all."

_____

"I have learned not frequently nor without necessity to say to any one or to write in a letter that I have no leisure, nor continually to excuse neglect of duties by alleging urgent occupation."

_____

"Accustom thyself carefully to attend to what is said by another and as much as possible try to be in the speaker's mind."

_____

"I have learned to receive from friends what are esteemed favors without being humbled or letting them pass unnoticed."

_____

"I have learned that it is possible for a man to live in a palace without wanting either guards or embroidered dresses, and to be content in a palace with a plank bed."

_____

"I have learned to work with my hands."

_____

"Do not speak of thy bodily ailments to those who visit thee when thou art sick."

_____

"The greatest part of what we say and do is really unnecessary. If a man takes this to heart he will have more leisure and less uneasiness."

_____

"Do every act in thy life as if it were the last."

_____

"Think of those things only which, if thou shouldst suddenly be asked, 'Pray, what is in thy mind?' thou mightest with perfect frankness lay open as the contents of thy mind."

_____

"A man must stand erect and not be held erect by others."

"Begin the morning by saying to thyself, 'I must rise now from my bed to do the work of a man.' Begin the morning by saying to thyself, 'I shall meet to-day with the busybody, the ungrateful, the arrogant, the deceitful, the envious, the unsocial; but I, who have seen the nature of the good that it is beautiful, and of the bad that it is ugly, and the nature of him that is wrong that it is akin to mine – I cannot be injured by one of them, nor can I be angry since he is my kinsman and I cannot hate him.' "

"We are made for co-operation like feet, hands, like eyelids, like the rows of the upper and lower teeth. Like a hand or foot cut off, such does a man make himself who does anything unsocial."

"What is good for the bee is good for the swarm."

"Reverence that which is best in the universe and in like manner reverence that which is best in thyself, and the one is at the same time as the other."

"Where a man can live, he can also live well; but he may have to live in a palace – well, then he can also live well in a palace."

"Man has sensations and appetites in common with animals. There remains that which is peculiar to man, to be contented with that which is appointed him and not to defy the divinity which is planted within his breast."

"Take me and place me where thou wilt, for there I shall keep my divine part tranquil."

"The pain which is intolerable carries us off, but that which lasts a long time is tolerable."

"The soul of the good is naked and is manifest through the body that surrounds it. There is no veil over a star."

"Be like the promontory against which the waves continually break; but it stands firm and tames the fury of the water around it."

"Live as on a mountain."

"The soul is a sphere illuminated by light, by which it sees the truth of all things and the truth that is in itself."

"I do my duty; other things trouble me not."

These are a few of the sayings of Marcus Aurelius. There are others like them—apples of gold in baskets of silver.

TODAY

So here hath been dawning
   Another blue day:
Think, wilt thou let it
   Slip useless away.

Out of Eternity
   This new day was born;
Into Eternity,
   At night, will return.

Behold it aforetimes
   No eye ever did;
So soon it for ever
   From all eyes is hid.

Here hath been dawning
   Another blue day:
Think, wilt thou let it
   Slip useless away.

—THOMAS CARLYLE.

Time's glory is to calm contending kings,
To unmask falsehood and bring truth to light,
To stamp the seal of time in aged things,
To wake the morn and sentinel the night,
To wrong the wronger till he render right,
To ruinate proud buildings with thy hours,
And smear with dust their glittering golden towers.

—SHAKESPEARE, *The Rape of Lucrice.*

ONE DEED OF GOOD

IF I might do one deed of good,
    One little deed before I die,
Or think one noble thought that should
    Hereafter not forgotten lie,
I would not murmur though I must
Be lost in Death's unnumbered dust.

The filmy wing, that wafts the seed
    Upon the careless wind to earth,
Lives only for a moment's deed,
    To find the germ fit place for birth;
For one swift moment of delight
It whirls,— then withers out of sight.

*A good man makes no noise over a good deed, but
passes on to another as a vine to bear grapes again
in season.*
            —MARCUS AURELIUS, Meditations

*It is a most mortifying reflection for a man to con-
sider what he has done, compared with what he
might have done.*
                 —SAMUEL JOHNSON

...learning is like mercury...

Learning is like mercury, one of the most powerful and excellent things in the world in skilful hands; in unskilful, the most mischievous.

The nicest constitutions of government are often like the finest pieces of clock-work, which, depending on so many motions, are therefore more subject to be out of order.

Every man has just as much vanity as he wants understanding.

Modesty, if it were to be recommended for nothing else, this were enough, that the pretending to little leaves a man at ease; whereas boasting requires perpetual labor to appear what he is not. If we have sense, modesty best proves it to others: if we have none, it best hides our want of it.

It is not so much the being exempt from faults as the having overcome them that is an advantage to us: it being with the follies of the mind as with the weeds of a field, which, if destroyed and consumed upon the place of their birth, enrich and improve it more than if none had ever sprung there.

To pardon those absurdities in ourselves which we cannot suffer in others is neither better nor worse than to be more willing to be fools ourselves than to have others so.

A man should never be ashamed to own he has been in the wrong, which is but saying, in other words, that he is wiser today than he was yesterday.

Our passions are like convulsive fits, which, though they make us stronger for the time, leave us weaker ever after.

To be angry is to revenge the fault of others upon ourselves.

A brave man thinks no one his superior who does him an injury; for he has it then in his power to make himself superior to the other by forgiving it.

To relieve the oppressed in the most glorious act a man is capable of; it is in some measure doing the business of God and Providence.

Superstition is the spleen of the soul.

What Tully says of war may be applied to disputing; it should be always so managed as to remember that the only end of it is peace: but generally true disputants are like true sportsmen, their whole delight is in the pursuit; and a disputant no more cares for the truth than the sportsman for the hare.

When men grow virtuous in their old age, they only make a sacrifice to God of the devil's leavings.

When we are young we are slavishly employed in procuring something whereby we may live comfortably when we grow old; and when we are old we perceive it is too late to live as we proposed.

We ought in humanity no more to despise a man for the misfortunes of the mind than for those of the body, when they are such as he cannot help. Were this thoroughly considered, we should no more laugh at one for having his brains cracked than for having his head broke.

A man of wit is not incapable of business, but above it. A sprightly, generous horse is able to carry a pack-saddle as well as an ass, but he is too good to be put to the drudgery.

Wherever I find a great deal of gratitude in a poor man, I take it for granted there would be as much generosity if he were a rich man.

When two people compliment each other with the choice of anything, each of them generally gets that which he likes least.

He who tells a lie is not sensible how great a task he undertakes; for he must be forced to invent twenty more to maintain that one.

Some people will never learn anything, for this reason, because they understand everything too soon.

The vanity of human life is like a river, constantly passing away, and yet constantly coming on.

WHAT ENDURES?

Nothing endures but personal qualities.

What do you think endures?
Do you think a great city endures"
Or a teeming manufacturing state? or a prepared
    constitution? or the best built steamships?
Or hotels of granite and iron? or any chef-d'oeuvres
    of engineering, forts, armaments?

Away! these are not to be cherish'd for themselves,
They fill their hour, the dancers dance, the musicians
    play for them,
The show passes, all does well enough of course,
All does very well till one flash of defiance.

A great city is that which has the greatest men
    and women,
If it be a few ragged huts it is still the greatest city
    in the whole world.

                —WALT WHITMAN

A REFLECTION AT SEA

See how, beneath the moonbeam's smile,
   Yon little billow heaves its breast,
And foams and sparkles for a while,
Then murmuring subsides to rest!

Thus man, the sport of bliss and care,
Rises on time's eventful sea,
And having swelled a moment there,
Thus melts into eternity.

                —THOMAS MOORE

GRAINS OF TRUTH

No woman hates a man for being in love with her; but many a woman hates a man for being a friend to her.

It is with narrow-souled people as with narrow-necked bottles, the less they have in them the more noise they make in pouring it out.

Get your enemies to read your works in order to mend them; for your friend is so much your second self that he will judge too like you.

There should be, methinks, as little merit in loving a woman for her beauty as in loving a man for his prosperity; both being equally subject to change.

The most positive men are the most credulous; since they most believe themselves, and advise most with the falsest flatterer and worst enemy, their own self-love.

An excuse is worse and more terrible than a lie; for an excuse is a lie guarded.

The wonder we often express at our neighbors keeping dull company would lessen if we reflected that most people seek companions less to be talked to than to talk.

It often happens that those are the best people whose characters have been most injured by slanders; as we usually find that to be the sweetest fruit which the birds have been pecking at.

The greatest things and the most praiseworthy that can be done for the public good are not what require great intellect, but great honesty: therefore for a politician to make a good record he needs only to be a man of common honesty well advised.

THE PIONEERS' BALL
by MARK TWAIN

IT WAS ESTIMATED that four hundred persons were present at the ball. The gentlemen wore the orthodox costume for such occasions, and the ladies were dressed the best they knew how. N. B.—Most of these ladies were pretty, and some of them absolutely beautiful. Four out of every five ladies present were pretty. The ratio at the Colfax party was two out of every five. I always keep the run of these things. While upon this department of the subject, I may as well tarry a moment and furnish you with descriptions of some of the most noticeable costumes.

Mrs. W. M. was attired in an elegant *pate de foi gras,* made expressly for her, and was greatly admired.

Miss S. had her hair done up. She was the center of attraction for the gentlemen, and the envy of all the ladies.

Miss G. W. was tastefully dressed in a *tout ensemble,* and was greeted with deafening applause wherever she went.

Mrs. C. N. was superbly arrayed in white kid gloves. Her modest and engaging manner accorded well with the unpretending simplicity of her costume, and caused her to be regarded with absorbing interest by every one.

The charming Miss M. M. B. appeared in a thrilling waterfall, whose exceeding grace and volume compelled the homage of pioneers and emigrants alike. How beautiful she was!

The queenly Mrs. L. B. was attractively attired in her new and beautiful false teeth, and the *bon jour* effect they naturally produced was heightened by her enchanting and well-sustained smile. The manner of this lady is charmingly pensive and melancholy, and her troops of admirers desired no greater happiness than to get on the scent of her sozodont-sweetened sighs and track her through her sinuous course among the gay and restless multitude.

Miss R. P., with that repugnance to ostentation in dress which is so peculiar to her, was attired in a simple white lace collar, fastened with a neat pearl-button solitaire. The fine contrast between the sparkling vivacity of her natural optic and the steadfast attentiveness of her placid glass eye was the subject of general and enthusiastic remark.

The radiant and sylph-like Mrs. T., late of your state, wore hoops. She showed to good advantage, and created a sensation wherever she appeared. She was the gayest of the gay.

Miss C. L. B. had her fine nose elegantly enameled, and the easy grace with which she blew it from time to time, marked her as a cultivated and accomplished woman of the world; its exquisitely modulated tone excited the admiration of all who had the happiness to hear it.

Being offended with Miss X., and our acquaintance having ceased prematurely, I will take this opportunity of observing to her that it is of no use for her to be slopping off to every ball that takes place, and flourishing around with a brass oyster-knife skewered through her waterfall, and smiling her sickly smile through her decayed teeth, with her dismal pug nose in the air. There is no use in it—she don't fool anybody. Everybody knows that she is old; everybody knows she is repaired (you might almost say built) with artificial bones and hair and muscles and things, from the ground up—put together scrap by scrap—and everybody knows, also, that all one would have to do would be to pull out her key-pin and she would go to pieces like a Chinese puzzle. There, now, my faded flower, take that paragraph home with you and amuse yourself with it; and if ever you turn your wart of a nose up at me again I will sit down and write something that will just make you rise up and howl.

FROM THE *Golden Era,* NOV. 26, 1865. [T. E.]

TO STIMULATE THOUGHT

He who offends against Heaven has none to whom he can pray.

When we see men of worth, we should think of becoming like them: when we see men of a contrary character, we should turn inward and examine ourselves.

I am not concerned that I have no office: I am concerned how I may fit myself for one. I am not concerned that I am not known: I seek to be worthy to be known.

The superior man thinks of virtue: the small man thinks of comfort. The superior man thinks of the sanctions of law: the small man thinks of the favors which he may receive.

What the superior man seeks is in himself: what the small man seeks is in others.

—LA ROCHEFOUCAULD

Aristotle was asked what were the advantages of learning. He replied, "It is an ornament to a man in prosperity, and a refuge to him in adversity."

A new race of men is springing up to govern the nation; they are the hunters after popularity, men ambitious not of the honor so much as of the profits of office—the demagogues, whose principles hang laxly upon them, and who follow not so much what is right as what leads to a temporary vulgar applause.

JOSEPH STORY, *Professor of Law at Harvard, 1829-1845*

"When he leaves our house, let us count our spoons." *Said of a man who claimed there was no distinction between virtue and vice.*

—SAMUEL JOHNSON

Articles of Friendship
Written in the 17th Century

I. Lest it may more quarrels breed,
I will never hear you read.

II. By disputing, I will never,
To convince you once endeavor.

III. When a paradox you stick to,
I will never contradict you.

IV. When I talk and you are heedless,
I will show no anger needless.

V. When your speeches are absurd,
I will ne'er object a word.

VI. When you furious argue wrong,
I will grieve and hold my tongue.

VII. Not a jest or humorous story
Will I ever tell before ye:
To be chidden for explaining,
When you quite mistake the meaning.

VIII. Never more will I suppose
You can taste my verse or prose.

IX. You no more at me shall fret,
While I teach and you forget.

X. You shall never hear me thunder,
When you blunder on and blunder.

XI. Show your poverty of spirit,
And in dress place all your merit;
Give yourself ten thousand airs:
That with me shall break no squares.

XII. Never will I give advice
Till you please to ask me thrice:
Which if you in scorn reject,
'Twill be just as I expect.
Thus we both shall have our ends,
And continue special friends.

A man cannot be said to succeed in this
life who does not satisfy one friend.

—THOREAU, *Winter*

GEMS, FROM BEN JOHNSON'S DISCOVERIES

Very few books contain as much wisdom in as little space as Ben Jonson's book of *Discoveries*. And yet, as we never hear it spoken of or quoted, it seems very clear that no one ever reads it. We grace our store-house of useful curiosities with one or two specimens of the bright golden ore hid in abundance in this unexplored mine. As the extracts are made as short as possible, the reader will observe that the words at the head of each are not always our author's, but often merely our own nomenclature for the gems in our little cabinet:

Fortune.—Ill-fortune never crushed that man whom good-fortune deceived not.

Self-reliance.—He knows not his own strength, that hath not met adversity.

Counsel.—No man is so foolish, but may give another good counsel sometimes; and no man is so wise, but may easily err, if he will take no other's counsel but his own.

True Wisdom.—Wisdom without honesty is mere craft and cozenage.

Discernment.—There are many that, with more ease, will find fault with what is spoken foolishly, than can give allowance to that wherein you are wise silently.

Stupidity.—A man cannot imagine that thing so foolish, or rude, but will find or enjoy an admirer.

Short-sightedness of Discontent.—If we would consider what our affairs are indeed, not what they are called, we should find more evils belonging to us, than happen to us.

Man, a Mimetic Animal.—I have considered our whole life is like a play: wherein every man, forgetful of himself, is in travail with expression of another.

Vice and Virtue.—If we will look with our understanding, and not our senses, we may behold virtue and beauty (though covered with rags) in their brightness; and vice and deformity so much the fouler, in having all the splendor of riches to gild them, or the false light of honor and power to help them.

Self-approval.—The worst opinion gotten for doing well should delight us.

Being above seeming.—I am glad when I see any man avoid the infamy of a vice; but to shun the vice itself were better.

The best Writer.—The order of God's creatures in themselves is not only admirable and glorious, but eloquent: then he who could apprehend the consequence of things in their truth, and utter his apprehensions as truly, were the best writer or speaker.

Poesy.—A dulcet and gentle philosophy, which leads on and guides us by the hand to action, with a ravishing delight, and incredible sweetness.

I bid him look into the lives of all men, as into a mirror, and to take example to himself from others.

—TERENCE

Example is a lesson that all men can read.

—GILBERT WEST, *Education*

We should endeavor to do something so that we may say that we have not lived in vain, that we may leave some impress of ourselves on the sands of time.

—NAPOLEON BONAPARTE

*Since truth and constancy are vain
Since neither love nor sense of pain,
Nor force of reason, can persuade,
Then let example be obey'd.*

—GEORGE GRANVILLE, *To Myra*

CORTES' FOLLOWERS AND THE DOVE

When Cortes was on his way to the New World, "their victuall waxed skant and their fresh water wanted, so that they prepared themselves to die. Some cursed their fortune, others asked mercy at God's hands, looking for death and to be eaten of the Carives. And in this time of tribulation came a dove flying to the ship, being on Good Friday at sunset, and sat him on the ship top: whereat they were all comforted, and took it for a miracle and good token, and some wept with joy, some said that God had sent the dove to comfort them, others said that land was near, and all gave hearty thanks to God directing their course that way that the dove flew."

—*Conquest of the West India.*

For Mercy has a human heart,
Pity a human face,
And Love, the human form divine,
And Peace, the human dress.

Then every man, of every clime,
That prays in his distress,
Prays to the human form divine,
Love, Mercy, Pity, Peace.

—WILLIAM BLAKE, *The Divine Image*

WHAT IS TIME?

What is time? The shadow on the dial, the striking of the clock, the running of the sand day and night, summer and winter, months, years, centuries — these are but arbitrary and outward signs, the measure of Time, not Time itself. Time is the life of the soul.

—LONGFELLOW, *Hyperion*

THERE IS A TIME FOR EVERYTHING

To everything there is a season, and a time to every purpose under heaven:
A time to be born and a time to die; a time to plant, and a time to pluck up that which is planted;
A time to kill, and a time to heal; a time to break down, and a time to build up;
A time to weep, and a time to laugh; a time to mourn, and a time to dance; . . .
A time to get and a time to lose; a time to keep, and a time to cast away;
A time to rend, and a time to sew; a time to keep silence and a time to speak;
A time to love, and a time to hate; a time of war, and a time of peace.

—ECCLESIASTES III, 1-8

THE MYSTERY OF TIME

That great mystery of Time, were there no other; the illimitable, silent never-resting thing called Time, rolling, rushing on, swift, silent, like an all-embracing ocean tide, on which we and all the Universe swim like exhalations, like apparitions which are, and then are not: this is forever very literally a miracle; a thing to strike us dumb — for we have no word to speak about it!

—CARLYLE, *Heroes and Hero Worship*

ON LIVING

To be honest, to be kind—to earn a little and to spend a little less, to make upon the whole a family happier for his presence, to renounce when that shall be necessary and not embittered, to keep a few friends, but these without capitulation—above all, on the same grim condition to keep friends with himself—here is a task for all that a man has of fortitude and delicacy.

— ROBERT LOUIS STEVENSON

There are two things to aim at in life: first, to get what you want; and after that to enjoy it. Only the wisest of mankind achieve the second.

— LOGAN SMITH, *Afterthoughts*

Life's all getting and giving,
I've only myself to give.
What shall I do for a living?
I've only one life to live.
End it? I'll not find another.
Spend it? But how shall I best?
Sure the wise plan is to live like a man
And Luck may look after the rest.

— RUDYARD KIPLING, *The Wishing-Caps*

All of the animals excepting man know that the principal business of life is to enjoy it.

— SAMUEL BUTLER

The fool with all his other thoughts, has this also: he is always getting ready to live.

— EPICURUS

And I though to myself, How nice it is
For me to live in a world like this,
Where things can happen and clocks can strike,
And none of the people are made alike.

—W. B. RANDS, *I Saw a New World*

TODAY

Two days have bothered men for years,
Have worried them with needless fears;
    But yesterday is past and done,
Tomorrow has not yet begun,
    So make the most of this one day,
Today is yours, so heed the way
    You use these hours — the deeds you do
Will mark the past and future, too.
    Today is yours, each sunbright hour,
Each passing storm and sudden shower;
    But you can face it, come what may,
For GOD is there to show the way.

Some say "tomorrow" never comes,
A saying oft thought right;
But if tomorrow never came,
No end were of "tonight."
The fact is this, time flies so fast,
That e'er we've time to say
"Tomorrow's come," presto! behold!
"Tomorrow" proves "Today."

SALUTATION OF THE DAWN
From The Sanscrit

Listen to the exhortation of the dawn!
Look to this day, for it is life —
The very life of life!
In its brief course lie all the verities
And realities of your existence;
The bliss of growth,
The glory of action,
The splendor of beauty;
For yesterday is but a dream,
And tomorrow is only a vision;
But today well-lived
Makes every yesterday a dream of happiness,
And every tomorrow a vision of hope.
Look well, therefore, to this day!
Such is the salutation of the dawn.

FOR WHAT IS LIFE?

For what is life, if measured by the space
    Not by the act?
Or masked man, if valued by his face
    Above his fact?
    Here's one outlived his peers,
    And told forth fourscore years;
He vexed time, and busied the whole state;
    Troubled both foes and friends;
    But ever to no ends;
What did this stirrer, but die late?
How well at twenty had he fallen or stood!
For three of his fourscore, he did no good.

It is not growing like a tree
    In bulk, doth make men better be;
Or standing long an oak, three hundred year,
To fall a log at last, dry, bald, and sear:
    A lily of a day
    Is fairer far in May
Although it fall and die that night;
It was the plant, and flower of light.
In small proportions we just beauties see;
And in short measures, life may perfect be.

               — BEN JONSON

*Life is an arrow — therefore you must know
what mark to aim at, how to use the bow —
Then draw it to the head, and let it go!*
        — HENRY VAN DYKE, *The Arrow.*

*Happiness is not a reward — it is a consequence.
Suffering is not a punishment — it is a result.*
              — INGERSOLL.

Life Is an End in Itself

The joy, the duty, and, I venture to add, the end of life. I speak only of this world, of course, and of the teachings of this world. I do not seek to trench upon the province of spiritual guides. But from the point of view of the world the end of life is life. Life is action, the use of one's powers. As to use them to their height is our joy and duty, so it is the one end that justifies itself. Until lately the best thing that I was able to think of in favor of civilization, apart from blind acceptance of the order of the universe, was that it made possible the artist, the poet, the philosopher, and the man of science. But I think that is not the greatest thing. Now I believe that the greatest thing is a matter that comes directly home to us all. When it is said that we are too much occupied with the means of living to live, I answer that the chief work of civilization is just that it makes the means of living more complex; that it calls for great and combined intellectual efforts, instead of simple, uncoördinated ones, in order that the crowd may be fed and clothed and housed and moved from place to place. Because more complex and intense intellectual efforts mean a fuller and richer life. They mean more life. Life is an end in itself, and the only question as to whether it is worth living is whether you have enough of it.

> Life is not dated merely by years. Events are sometimes the best calendars.
> — BENJAMIN DISRAELI, *Venetia*.

> It is with life as with a play: what matters is not how long it is, but how good it is.
> — SENECA.

Strong men greet war, tempest, hard times. They wish "to tread the floors of hell, with necessities as hard as iron."

...There is a destiny that makes us brothers

There is a destiny that makes us brothers:
    None goes his way alone:
All that we send into the lives of others
    Comes back into our own.

I care not what his temples or his creeds,
    One thing holds firm and fast—
That into his fateful heap of days and deeds
    The soul of a man is cast.

My brother kneels, so saith Kabir,
To stone and brass in heathen-wise,
But in my brother's voice I hear
My own unanswered agonies.
His God is as his fates assign,
His prayer is all the world's—and mine.

    —RUDYARD KIPLING, *The Prayer*

The world has a thousand creeds, and never
    a one have I;
Nor church of my own, though a million
    spires are pointing the way on high.
But I float on the bosom of faith, that bears
    me along like a river;
And the lamp of my soul is alight with love,
    for life, and the world, and the Giver.

    —ELLA WHEELER WILCOX, *Heresy*

Creeds for the credulous; but not for me,
I choose to keep a mind alert and free,
Not Faith but Truth I set me for a goal:
Toward that shining mark, God, speed thee, Soul.

    —FRANK DEMPSTER SHERMAN, *The Goal*

FOUR KINDS OF MEN

There are four kinds of men:
He who knows not and knows not he knows not:
    he is a fool — shun him;
He who knows not and knows he knows not:
    he is simple — teach him;
He who knows and knows not he knows:
    he is asleep — wake him;
He who knows and knows he knows:
    he is wise — follow him.

                 —DARIUS THE PERSIAN

When a man's knowledge is not in order, the more of it he has the greater will be his confusion.

    —HERBERT SPENCER, *The Study of Sociology*

Knowledge is a comfortable and necessary retreat and shelter for us in an advanced age; and if we do not plant it while young, it will give us no shade when we grow old.

                 —LORD CHESTERFIELD

Knowledge is of two kinds. We know a subject ourselves or we know where we can find information upon it.

                 —SAMUEL JOHNSON

It is the peculiarity of knowledge that those who really thirst for it always get it.

WHAT ARE THE HALCYON DAYS?

Poets and novelists often refer to certain periods in life's calendar, such that are expressive of tranquility and happiness, as "Halcyon Days."

This familiar phrase has its origin in an ancient fable, that during the seven days preceding and the seven days following the shortest day in the year, while the halcyon bird or kingfisher was breeding, the sea was always calm, and might be navigated in perfect security by the mariner. According to poetic fiction, the bird was represented as hatching her eggs on a floating nest in the midst of the waters.

———

I can tell you what that bird was—a kingfisher, the celebrated halcyon of the ancients about which so many tales are told. It lives on fish which it catches in the manner you saw. It builds in holes in the banks, is a shy, retiring bird, never to be seen far from the stream where it inhabits.

—JOHN AIKEN

———

This Was His Halcyon Day

A little wan-faced boy guided a plow to and fro all day across a clean, sweet field. With large head and small body, stumbling in and out of the furrow, now he held the plow, and now the plow held him. And by his side a rosy, black-eyed girl walked with him over the clods.

As they went together back and forth and back again in the sunshine, the Lark swung down the breeze, and met the smell of fresh-turned earth, and the jingle of the blackbirds in the maples; and he saw the boy and girl were in another world. For, as she tramped it up and down beside her brother, urging the old horse, that the whole forenoon she read aloud to him, in her clear, young voice, out of a magic book the *Song of Hiawatha*.

GELETT BURGESS, *Editor*

THE PERIPATETIC PRESS

The newspapers of Paris, submitted to the censorship of the press, in 1815, announced in the following terms, Bonaparte's departure from the Isle of Elba, his march across France, and his entry into the French Capital: —9th March —The Cannibal has escaped from his den. 10th—The Corsican ogre has just landed at Cape Juan. 11th—The Tiger has arrived at Gap. 12th—The Monster has passed the night at Grenoble. 13th—The Tyrant has crossed Lyons. 14th—The Usurper is directing his course towards Dijon, but the brave and loyal Burgundians have risen in a body, and they surround him on all sides. 18th—Bonaparte is sixty leages from the Capital; he has had skill enough to escape from the hands of his pursuers. 19th—Bonaparte advances rapidly, but he will never enter Paris. 20th—To-morrow, Napoleon will be under our ramparts. 21st—The Emperor is at Fontainebleau. 22nd—His Imperial and Royal Majesty last evening made his entrance into his Palace of the Tuileries, amidst the joyous acclamations of an adoring and faithful people.

Perhaps an editor might . . . divide his paper into four chapters heading the first, Truths; second, Probabilities; third, Possibilities; fourth, Lies.
—THOMAS JEFFERSON, *Writings*

Were it left to me to decide whether we should have a government without newspapers, or newspapers without a government, I should not hesitate a moment to prefer the latter.
—THOMAS JEFFERSON, *Writings*

There is no playing fast and loose with the truth, in any game, without growing the worse for it.
— CHARLES DICKENS—*Little Dorrit*

FORBEARANCE

Hast thou named all the birds without a gun?
Loved the wood-rose, and left it on its stalk?
At rich men's tables eaten bread and pulse?
Unarmed, faced danger with a heart of trust?
And loved so well a high behavior,
In man or maid, that thou from speech refrained,
Nobility more nobly to repay?
O, be my friend, and teach me to be thine!

—RALPH WALDO EMERSON.

I count him braver who overcomes his desires than him who conquers his enemies; for the hardest victory is the victory over self.

—ARISTOTLE

Thrice noble is the man who of himself is king.

—PHINEAS FLETCHER

There is a victory and defeat—the first and best of victories, the lowest and worst of defeats—which each man gains or sustains at the hands, not of another, but of himself.

—PLATO, *Laws*

Man who man would be, must rule the empire of himself; in it must be supreme, establishing his throne on vanquished will, quelling the anarchy of hopes and fears, being himself along.

—SHELLEY, *Political Greatness*

WHAT IS CHARITY

It is Silence—when your words would hurt.
It is Patience—when your neighbor's curt.
It is Deafness—when a scandal flows,
It is Thoughtfulness—for others' woes.
It is Promptness—when stern duty calls,
It is Courage—when misfortune falls.

Though I speak with the tongues of men and of angels, and
have not charity, I am become as sounding brass or a tinkling cymbal. And though I have the gift of prophecy, and
understand all mysteries, and all knowledge; and though
I have all faith, so that I could remove mountains, and
have not charity, I am nothing. And though I bestow all
my goods to feed the poor, and though I give my body to
be burned, and have not charity, it profit me nothing.
Charity suffereth long and is kind; charity envieth not;
charity vaunteth not itself, is not puffed up, doth not be-
have itself unseemly, seeketh not her own, is not easily
provoked, thinketh no evil; Rejoiceth not in iniquity, but
rejoiceth in the truth. Beareth all things, believeth all
things, hopeth all things, endureth all things.

—I CORINTHIANS, 1-7.

I deem it the duty of every man to devote a certain portion
of his income for charitable purposes; and that it is his
further duty to see it so applied as to do the most good of
which it is capable. This I believe to be best insured by
keeping within the circle of his own inquiry and information the subjects of distress to whose relief his contribu-
tions should be applied.

—THOMAS JEFFERSON, *Writings*.

He who bestows his goods upon the poor,
Shall have as much again, and ten times more.

—JOHN BUNYAN, *The Pilgrim's Progress*.

FOLK-LORE OF PLAYING CARDS

DIAMONDS

King • A man of very fair complexion; quick to anger, but soon appeased.

Queen • A very fair woman, fond of gaiety, and a coquette.

Knave • A selfish and deceitful relative; fair and false.

Ten • Money. Success in honorable business.

Nine • A roving disposition, combined with honorable and successful adventure in foreign lands.

Eight • A happy prudent marriage, though rather late in life.

Seven • Satire. Scandal. Unpleasant business matters.

Six • Marriage early in life, succeeded by widowhood.

Five • Unexpected news, generally of a good kind.

Four • An unfaithful friend. A secret betrayed.

Trey • Domestic troubles, quarrels and unhappiness.

Deuce • A clandestine engagement. A card of caution.

Ace • A wedding ring. An offer of marriage.

CLUBS

King • A dark complexioned man, though not so dark as the king of spades; upright, true, and affectionate.

Queen • A woman of the same complexion, agreeable, genteel, and witty.

Knave • A sincere, but rather hasty-tempered friend.

Ten • Unexpected wealth, through the death of a relative. A fat sorrow.

Nine • Danger caused by drunkenness. A card of caution.

Eight • Danger from covetousness. A card of caution.

Seven • A prison. Danger arising from the opposite sex. A card of caution.

Six • Competence by hard-working industry.

Five • A happy, though not wealthy marriage.

Four • Danger of misfortunes caused by inconstancy, or capricious temper. A card of caution.

Trey • Quarrels. Or in reference to time may signify three years, three months, three weeks, or three days. It also denotes that a person will be married more than once.

Deuce • Vexation, disappointment.

Ace • A letter.

HEARTS

King • A fair, but not very fair, complexioned man; good natured, but rather obstinate, and, when angered, not easily appeased.

Queen • A woman of the same complexion as the king; faithful, prudent, and affectionate.

Knave • An unselfish relative. A sincere friend.

Ten • Health and happiness, with many children.

Nine • Wealth. High position in society. The wish-card.

Eight • Fine clothes. Pleasure. Mixing in good society. Going to balls, theatres, etc.

Seven • Many good friends.

Six • Honorable courtship.

Five • A present.

Four • Domestic troubles caused by jealousy.

Trey • Poverty, shame and sorrow, caused by imprudence. A card of caution.

Deuce • Success in life, position in society, and a happy marriage, attained by virtuous discretion.

Ace • The house of the person consulting the decrees of fate.

SPADES

King • A man of very dark complexion, ambitious and unscrupulous.

Queen • A very dark complexioned woman, of malicious disposition. A widow.

Knave • A lawyer. A person to be shunned.

Ten • Disgrace; crime; imprisonment. Death on the scaffold. A card of caution.

Nine • Grief; ruin; sickness; death.

Eight • Great danger from imprudence. A card of caution.

Seven • Unexpected poverty caused by the death of a relative. A lean sorrow.

Six • A child. To the unmarried a card of caution.

Five • Great danger from giving way to bad temper. A card of caution.

Four • Sickness.

Trey • A journey by land. Tears.

Deuce • A removal.

Ace • Death; malice; a duel; a general misfortune.

EDUCATION

Whom, then, do I call educated? First, those who control circumstances instead of being mastered by them, those who meet all occasions manfully and act in accordance with intelligent thinking, those who are honorable in all dealings, who treat good-naturedly persons and things that are disagreeable; and furthermore, those who hold their pleasures under control and are not overcome by misfortune; finally, those who are not spoiled by success.

— SOCRATES

By far the most important bill in our whole code, is that for the diffusion of knowledge among the people. No other sure foundation can be devised for the preservation of freedom and happiness.

— THOMAS JEFFERSON.

I desire to see the time when education, and by its means, morality, sobriety, enterprise and industry, shall become much more general than at present.

— ABRAHAM LINCOLN.

Next in importance to freedom and justice is popular education, without which neither freedom nor justice can be permanently maintained.

— JAMES A. GARFIELD.

WALT WHITMAN TELLS ABOUT HIMSELF

from Leaves of Grass, DAVID MCKAY

I am of old and young, of the foolish as much as the wise;
Regardless of others, ever regardful of others,
Maternal as well as paternal, a child as well as a man,
Stuff'd with the stuff that is coarse, and stuff'd with the
  stuff that is fine;
One of the Great Nation, the nation of many nations, the
  smallest the same, and the largest the same;
A southerner soon as a northerner – a planter nonchalant
  and hospitable, down by the Oconee I live;
A Yankee, bound by my own way, ready for trade, my
  joints the limberest joints on earth, and the sternest
  joints on earth;
A Kentuckian, walking the vale of the Elkhorn, in my
  deer-skin leggings – a Louisianian or Georgian;
A boatman over lakes or bays, or along coasts – a Hoosier,
  Badger, Buckeye;
At home on Canadian snow-shoes, or up in the bush, or
  with fishermen off Newfoundland;
At home in the fleet of ice-boats, sailing with the rest and
  tacking;
At home on the hills of Vermont, or in the woods of
  Maine, or the Texan ranch;
Comrade of Californians – comrade of free north-western-
  ers, (loving their big proportions;)
Comrade of raftsmen and coalmen – comrade of all who
  shake hands and welcome to drink and meat;
A learner with the simplest, a teacher of the thought-
  fullest;
A novice beginning, yet experient of myriads of seasons;
Of every hue and caste am I, of every rank and religion;
A farmer, mechanic, artist, gentleman, sailor, quaker;
A prisoner, fancy-man, rowdy, lawyer, physician, priest.
I resist anything better than my own diversity;
I breathe   the air, but leave plenty after me,
And am not stuck up, and am in my place.

The satisfaction of doing a good turn is reward enough

He who receives a good turn should never forget it: he who does one should never remember it. — *Charron.*

. . . One man, when he has done a service to another, is ready to set it down to his account as a favor conferred. Another is not ready to do this, but still in his own mind he thinks of the man as his debtor, and he knows what he has done. A third in a manner does not even know what he has done, *but he is like a vine which has produced grapes, and seeks for nothing more after it has once produced its proper fruit.* As a horse when he has run, a dog when he has caught the game, a bee when it has made its honey, so a man when he has done a good act does not call out for others to come and see, but he goes on to another act, as a vine goes on to produce again the grapes in season. Must a man, then, be one of these, who in a manner acts thus without observing it? Yes.—*Marcus Aurelius.*

BE USEFUL

Be useful where thou livest, that they may
Both want and wish thy pleasing presence still.
   —Find out men's wants and will,
And meet them there, All worldly joys go less
To the one joy of doing kindnesses.

              —GEORGE HERBERT.

So many Gods, so many creeds,
So many paths that wind and wind;
While yet the art of being kind
Is all the sad world needs.

            Ella Wheeler Wilcox.

Four good habits leading to Success

Here are four good habits—punctuality, accuracy, steadiness, and decision. Without the first of these, time is wasted; without the second, mistakes, the most hurtful to our own credit and interest, and that of others, may be committed; without the third, nothing can be well done; and without the fourth, opportunities of great advantage are lost, which it is impossible to recall.

"I owe everything in the world to being always a quarter of an hour beforehand."—*Lord Nelson.*

A Strong Man Needs a Challenge

Almost everything worth knowing we teach ourselves after leaving school. But the discipline of school is invaluable in teaching the important lesson of self-control. Self-denial and self-control are the necessary postulates of all moral excellence. A man who will take the world easily will never take it grandly. To lie in the lap of luxury may be the highest enjoyment of what a feeble character is capable; but a strong man must have something difficult to do. Moreover, the happiness of the human race does not consist in our being devoid of passions, but in our learning to control them.— *Prof. J. S. Blackie.*

The poorest education that teaches self-control is better than the best that neglects it.—*Sterling.*

There never has been, and cannot be, a good life without self-control; apart from self-control, no good life is imaginable. The attainment of goodness must begin with that.

—Tolstoi

CHARACTER AND REPUTATION

Human life is character-building; for remember that character means exactly what we are, while reputation is only what other people think we are. Every man builds his own character.—*Cuyler.*

Reputation has its uses as a stimulus. It is not of nearly so much account as character, to be sure; for our reputation is only what people think we are, while our character is what we are. But there is one way by which we can make of our reputations—and we all have more than one—valuable helpers. A shrewdly thoughtful business man has told how, in this advice: "Be what your friends think you are; avoid being what your enemies say you are." *There* is a sure way to justify our friends and to confound our enemies—and nobody gets hurt by it.

THE LANGUAGE OF FRIENDS

We don't want arguments from our friends; we want sympathies, sensibilities—emotional bonds—the right person's silence is worth more for companionship than the wisest talk in the world from anybody else. It isn't your mind that is needed here, or what you know; it is your heart and what you feel.

Silence is the ambrosial night in the intercourse of friends, in which their sincerity is recruited and takes deeper root. The language of friends is not words, but meanings. It is an intelligence above language.—*H. D. Thoreau.*

In friendship—ev'n thought meets thought ere from the lips
  it part,
And each warm wish springs mutual from the heart.

—*Pope.*

CIRCUMSTANCES

There is a certain parallel between the relation of the soul to circumstances and that of the flower to the mineral kingdom. That small brown object, the seed, looking no better than a mineral itself, has somewhere concealed within it a distinct intention of becoming a rose. To this end it works steadily upward. It uses earth and water, air and sunshine, when it can, strives to ignore them when it cannot, resists them when it must; and, with the ordinary chances, becomes a rose in due time. It is a miraculous proceeding, a thing that we should know with absolute certainty could not happen, if we did not know that it does!

Surely, if a human being has only as much real or apparent power of moulding or subduing circumstances as an acorn or other seed, it would be wise to study certain aspects of his relation to them. But some of us hold that he has infinitely more power, not only of adapting the circumstances of time and space, but of fulfilling his own life-purpose apart from them, in a world they cannot enter.—*May Kendall.*

Man is not the creature of circumstances, circumstances are the creatures of men. We are free agents, and man is more powerful than matter.

—BENJAMIN DISRAELI, *Vivian Grey*

I don't believe in circumstances. The people who get on in this world are the people who get up and look for the circumstances they want.

—BERNARD SHAW, *Mrs. Warren's Profession*

RONDEL OF PERFECT FRIENDSHIP:

FRIEND of my soul, forever true,
   What do we care for flying years,
   Unburdened all by doubts or fears;
Trusting what naught can e'er subdue?

Fate leads! Her path is out of view;
   Nor time nor distance interferes.
Friend of my soul, forever true,
   What do we care for flying years?

For, planted when the world was new
   In other lives, in other spheres,
   Our love to-day a bud appears,—
Not yet the blossom's perfect hue,
Friend of my soul, forever true!

*There is nothing that is meritorious but virtue
and friendship; and, indeed, friendship is only
a part of virtue.*
                              —ALEXANDER POPE

NEVER YET

Was noble man but made ignoble talk.
He makes no friend who never made a foe.
                              —TENNYSON

Friends are like melons; shall I tell you why?
To find one good you must a hundred try.
                              — CLAUDE MERMET

*People who have warm friends are healthier and
happier than those who have none. A single real friend
is a treasure worth more than gold or precious stones.
Money can buy many things, good and evil. All the
wealth of the world could not buy you a friend or
pay you for the loss of one.*

Neither Time Nor Money Would Make You Happier

What are thou Freedom? Oh could slaves
Answer from their living graves
This demand, tyrants would flee
Like a dim dream's imagery!
Thou art Justice—ne'er for gold
May thy righteous laws be sold,
As laws are in England: thou
Shield'st alike high and low.
Thou art Peace – never by thee
Would blood and treasure wasted be
As tyrants wasted them when all
Leagued to quench thy flame in Gaul!
Thou art Love: the rich have kist
Thy feet and like him following Christ
Given their substance to be free
And through the world have followed thee.

—SHELLEY

As for a little more money and a little more time, why it's ten to one, if either one or the other would make you one whit happier. If you had more time, it would be sure to hang heavily. It is the working man who is the happy man. Man was made to be active, and he is never so happy as when he is so. It is the idle man who is the miserable man. What comes of holidays, and far too often of sight-seeing, but evil? Half the harm that happens is on those days. And, as for money – Don't you remember the old saying, "Enough is as good as a feast?" Money never made a man happy yet, nor will it. There is nothing in its nature to produce happiness. The more a man has, the more he wants. Instead of its filling a vacuum, it makes one. If it satisfies one want, it doubles and trebles that want another way. That was a true proverb of the wise man, rely upon it: "Better is little with the fear of the Lord, than great treasure, and trouble therewith."

—FRANKLIN

ELDORADO

Gaily bedight,
A gallant knight,
In sunshine and in shadow,
Had journeyed long,
Singing a song,
In search of Eldorado.

But he grew old—
This knight so bold—
And o'er his heart a shadow
Fell as he found
No spot of ground
That looked like Eldorado

And, as his strength
Failed him at length,
He met a pilgrim shadow—
"Shadow," said he,
"Where can it be—
This land of Eldorado?"

"Over the Mountains
Of the Moon,
Down the Valley of the Shadow,
Ride, boldly ride,"
The shade replied,—
"If you seek for Eldorado."

—EDGAR ALLAN POE

As much of heaven is visible as we have eyes to see.
—WILLIAM WINTER

THE ARROW AND THE SONG

I shot an arrow into the air;
It fell to earth, I knew not where:
For, so swiftly it flew, the sight
Could not follow it in its flight.

I breathed a song into the air;
It fell to earth, I know not where:
For who has sight so keen and strong,
That it can follow the flight of song?

Long, long afterward, in an oak
I found the arrow, still unbroke;
And the song, from beginning to end,
I found again in the heart of a friend.

—HENRY WADSWORTH LONGFELLOW.

NATURAL PIETY

My heart leaps up when I behold
    A rainbow in the sky:
So was it when my life began,
So is it now I am a man,
So be it when I shall grow old,
    Or let me die!
The Child is father of the Man:
And I could wish my days to be
Bound each to each by natural piety.

—WILLIAM WORDSWORTH

Bits of Knowledge That Will Do You No Good — But May Interest You

Memnon, the Egyptian, invented the letters, in the year 1822, *before* Christ.

The Alexandrian library, consisting of 400,000 valuable books, burned by accident, B. C. 52.

Glass was invented in England by Benalt, a monk, A. D. 400.

Paper made of cotton rags was in use, 1000 A. D.; that of linen rags in 1170.

Musical notes were invented, 1070.

Glass windows began to be used in private houses in England in 1180.

Surnames began to be used, first among the nobility, in 1200.

The houses of London and other cities in England, France, and Germany, still thatched with straw in 1233.

Tallow candles were so great a luxury, that splinters of wood were used for lights, 1298.

Gunpowder and guns first invented by Swartz, a monk of Cologne, 1340; Edward 3rd had four pieces of cannon, which contributed to gain him victory in the battle of Cressy, 1346; bombs and mortars were invented in the same year.

Cards invented in France for the king's amusement in 1391.

About 1430, Laurentius, of Haarlem, invented the art of Printing, which he practiced with separate wooden types. Guttenburg afterwards.

THE NIGHT HAS A THOUSAND EYES

THE night has a thousand eyes,
And the day but one;
Yet the light of the bright world dies
With the dying sun.

The mind has a thousand eyes.
And the heart but one;
Yet the light of a whole
life dies
When love is done.

THE ANGELUS

"Softly the Angelus sounded, and over the roofs of the
village
Columns of pale blue smoke, like clouds of incense
ascending,
Rose from a hundred hearths, the homes of peace and
contentment.
Thus dwelt together in love those simple Acadian farmers,—
Dwelt in the love of God and of man. Alike were they
free from
Fear, that reigns with the tyrant, and envy, the vice of
republics.
Neither locks had they to their doors, nor bars to their
windows;
But their dwellings were open as day and the hearts of
the owners;
There the richest was poor, and the poorest lived in
abundance."
— HENRY WADSWORTH LONGFELLOW, *Evangeline*

THE LAST WORD

There is one form which persistency takes that is peculiarly trying: I mean that persistency of opinion which deems it necessary to stop and raise an argument in self-defense, on the slightest personal criticism. . . . Love of the last word has made more bitterness in families than it is worth. A thousand little differences of this kind would drop to the ground if either party would let them drop. . . . Are they worth ill-tempered words, such as are almost sure to grow out of a discussion? Are they worth throwing away peace and love for? Are they worth the destruction of the only fair ideal left on earth—a quiet, happy home? Better let the most unjust statements pass in silence than risk one's temper in a discussion upon them.—*H. Beecher Stowe.*

From sharp words and wits men pluck no fruit;
And gathering thorns they shake the tree at the root.

—SWINBURNE

She dealt her pretty words like blades,
As glittering they shone,
And every one unbared a nerve
Or wantoned with a bone.

—EMILY DICKINSON, *Poems*

BUILD YOUR CASTLES ON TRUTH

There are a good many people who build castles in the air, cloud-capped, and live in hovels. . . . There is the castle of joy—the castle some call personal happiness, others, an ideal harmony between the self and the environment. Whatever we call it, we all long for it. It is not perhaps the loftiest castle, but it is full of exquisite surprises, with orchards and rose-gardens, and everywhere a sense of home. Within its walls we are glad at heart, with a gladness that does not pall. We accomplish noble work, and do not season it with blunders. There is a wonderful charm about us, and we are rich in friends, also we are surpremely necessary to the people we love best. It is easy to be good in that castle, and our good-ness becomes phenomenal: we mellow like sun-kissed peaches. Our true selves are set free, and God and man have a chance of seeing what we really are like.

Meanwhile, in daily life, we sit in desolation, and say that it is quite impossible to build up real happiness out of the little things that surround us. Other people have the great things, the gifts and opportunities, and human love and recognition, poured out in fullest measure. These are the porphyry, marble, and granite: we are left with rubble and clay.

It is a mistake. We are never forced back from the great things upon the little things, but we are being forced back perpetually from the little things upon the greatest things of all. If we open our eyes and see, nothing is really wanting, except the resolve to build.

> Is it not strange that desire should
> so many years outlive performance?
> —SHAKESPEARE II HENRY IV

ENTHUSIASM

There is a great adaptive power in human nature. The mind is wonderfully adjustive to different conditions; but you will not get the best results until your mind is settled, until you are resolved not only to like your work, but also to do it in the spirit of a master and not in that of a slave. Resolve that, whatever you do, you will like it; that you will bring the whole man to it; that you will fling the whole weight of your being into it; and that you will do it in the spirit of a conqueror, and so get the lesson and power out of it which come only to the conqueror.

Enthusiasm is one of the most powerful engines of success. When you do a thing, do it with your might. Put your whole soul into it. Stamp it with your own personality. Be active, be energetic, be enthusiastic and faithful, and you will accomplish your object. Nothing great was ever achieved without enthusiasm.

Every great and commanding moment in the annals of the world is the triumph of some enthusiasm.
—RALPH WALDO EMERSON

His rash fierce blaze of riot cannot last,
For violent fires soon burn out themselves;
Small showers last long but sudden storms are short;
He tires betimes that spurs too fast betimes.
—SHAKESPEARE, *Richard II*

Enthusiasm is that temper of the mind in which the imagination has got the better of the judgment.
—BISHOP WARBURTON

WHEN LOVE IS KIND

When Love is kind,
Cheerful and free,
Love's sure to find
Welcome from me!

But when Love brings
Heartache or pang,
Tears and such things—
Love may go hang!

If Love can sigh
For one alone,
Well pleased am I
To be that one.

But should I see
Love giv'n to rove
To two or three,
Then—good-bye, Love!

Love must, in short,
Keep fond and true,
Through good report,
And evil too.

Else, here I swear,
Young Love may go,
For aught I care—
To Jericho.

THOMAS MOORE (1779-1852)

Love is the emblem of eternity: it confounds all notion of time: effaces all memory of a beginning, all fear of an end.

—MADAME DE STAEL, *Corinne*

PUBLIC OPINION
ABHORS INEQUALITY

Our government rests in public opinion. Whoever can change public opinion can change the government practically just so much. Public opinion, on any subject, always has a central idea, from which all its minor thoughts radiate. That central idea in our political public opinion at the beginning was, and until recently has continued to be, the equality of men. And although it has always submitted patiently to whatever of inequality there seemed to be as matter of actual necessity, its constant working has been a steady progress toward the practical equality of all men.

I traversed a dominion
Whose spokesmen spake out strong
Their purpose and opinion
Through pulpit, press, and song . . .
I saw, in web unbroken,
Its history outwrought
Not as the loud had spoken,
But as the mute had thought.
— THOMAS HARDY, *Mute Opinion.*

I know where there is more wisdom than is found in Napoleon, Voltaire, or all the ministers present and to come—in public opinion.
— TALLEYRAND.

Singularity in right hath ruined many: happy those who are convinced of the general opinion.
— BEN FRANKLIN.

"...the world will little note, nor long remember what we say here, but it can never forget what they did here."

GEORGE WASHINGTON'S BENEDICTION
TO HIS ARMIES

"It only remains for the Commander in Chief to address himself once more, and for the last time, to the Armies of the United States, and to bid them an affectionate—a long farewell.

"It is universally acknowledged, that the enlarged prospects of happiness opened by the establishment of our independence, almost exceed the power of description; and shall not the brave men who have contributed so essentially to this inestimable acquisition, retiring victorious from the field of war to the field of agriculture, participate in all the blessings which have been obtained? In such a republic, who will exclude them from the rights of citizens, and the fruits of their labors? To these hardy soldiers who are actuated by the spirit of adventure, the fisheries will afford an ample and profitable employment; and the fertile regions of the west will yield a most happy asylum to these who, fond of domestic enjoyment, are seeking for personal independence.

"The Commander in Chief conceives little is now wanting to enable the soldiers to change the military character into that of the citizen; but that steady and decent tenor of behavior which has generally distinguished not only the army under his immediate command, but the different detachments and separate armies, through the course of the war—from their good sense and prudence, he anticipates the happiest consequences—and, while he congratulates them on the glorious occasion which renders their services in the field no longer necessary, he wishes to express the strong obligations he feels himself under, for the assistance he has received from every class, and in every instance. To the various branches of the army, the general takes this last and solemn opportunity of professing his inviolable attachment and friendship—he wishes more than bare professions were in his power—that he was really able to be useful to them in future life. And, being now to conclude these his last public orders, to take his ultimate leave, in a short time, of the military character, and to bid a final adieu to the armies he has so long had the honor to command, he can only again offer, in their behalf, his recommendations to their grateful country, and his prayers to the GOD of ARMIES. May ample justice be done them here, and may the choicest of heaven's favors both here and hereafter attend those, who, under the divine auspices, have secured innumerable blessings for others! With these wishes and this benediction, the Commander in Chief is about to retire from service. The curtain of separation will soon be drawn, and the military scene, to him, will be closed forever."

> *Whoever fights, whoever falls,*
> *Justice conquers evermore, . . .*
> *and he who battles on her side,*
> *God, though he were ten times slain,*
> *Crowns him victor glorified,*
> *Victor over death and pain.*
> —RALPH WALDO EMERSON: *Voluntaries.*

> *Render therefore to all their dues; tribute*
> *to whom tribute is due; custom to whom custom; fear to whom fear; honor to whom honor.*
> ROMANS XIII, 7

AMERICA AS SEEN BY ITS PRESIDENTS

Quoted from THIS WEEK *Magazine*

GEORGE WASHINGTON   *1789-1797*

"The name of American . . . must always exalt the just pride of patriotism. . . . The independence and liberty you possess are the work of joint councils and joint efforts, of common dangers, sufferings and successes."

JOHN ADAMS   *1797-1801*

"I must study politics and war, that my sons may have liberty to study mathematics and philosophy . . . in order to give their children the right to study painting, poetry, music."

THOMAS JEFFERSON   *1801-1809*

"The new circumstances under which we are placed call for new words, new phrases, and for the transfer of old words to new objects. An American dialect will therefore be formed."

JAMES MADISON   *1809-1817*

"The face of our country everywhere presents the evidence of laudable enterprise . . . In the extension of manufactures . . . we behold a rapid diminution of our dependence on foreign supplies."

JAMES MONROE   *1817-1825*

"The emigrants . . . although of different political parties and of different religious sects . . . all flew from persecution, in pursuit of liberty, and they inculcated that sentiment on their descendants."

JOHN QUINCY ADAMS   *1825-1829*

"America, in the assembly of nations . . . has invariably . . . held forth the hand of honest friendship. . . . She has uniformly spoken among them . . . the language of equal liberty, equal justice and equal rights."

ANDREW JACKSON   *1829-1837*

"As long as our Government is administered for the good of the people, and is regulated by their will . . . it will be worth defending."

MARTIN VAN BUREN   *1837-1841*

"The effects of distance have been averted by the inventive genius of our people, developed and fostered by the spirit of our institutions."

WILLIAM HENRY HARRISON   *1841-1841*

"Of all the great interests that appertain to our country, that of Union . . . is by far the most important, since it is the only true and sure guaranty of all others."

JOHN TYLER   *1841-1845*

"Let it, then, be henceforth proclaimed to the world, that man's conscience was created free; that he is no longer accountable to his fellow man for his religious opinions, being responsible therefor only to his God."

JAMES K. POLK   *1845-1849*

"While the people of other countries are struggling to establish free institutions, under which man may govern himself, we are in the actual enjoyment of them—a rich inheritance from our fathers."

ZACHARY TAYLOR   *1849-1850*

"Sixty years have elapsed since the establishment of this Government . . . and the United States presents to the world the most stable and permanent Government on earth."

MILLARD FILLMORE   *1850-1853*

"The ability to produce every necessary of life renders us independent in war as well as in peace."

FRANKLIN PIERCE   *1853-1857*

"While men inhabiting different parts of this vast continent cannot be expected to hold the same opinions . . . they can unite in a common object and sustain common principles."

JAMES BUCHANAN   *1857-1861*

"We shall best promote the prosperity of the new States and Territories by furnishing them with a hardy and independent race of honest and industrious citizens."

ABRAHAM LINCOLN   *1861-1865*

"Fellow-citizens, we cannot escape history. We . . . will be remembered in spite of ourselves. . . . The fiery trial through which we pass will light us down, in honor or dishonor, to the latest generation."

ANDREW JOHNSON   *1865-1869*

"It is the only government suited to our condition; but we have never sought to impose it on others, and we have consistently followed the advice of Washington to recommend it only by its careful preservation."

ULYSSES S. GRANT   *1869-1877*

"Our republican institutions were regarded as experiments up to the breaking out of the rebellion. . . . Now our people have proven themselves to be the most formidable in war of any nationality."

RUTHERFORD B. HAYES   *1877-1881*

"It is vain to hope for the success of a free government without the means of insuring the intelligence of those who are the source of power."

JAMES A. GARFIELD   *1881-1881*

"To all our means of culture is added the powerful incentive to personal ambition . . . No post of honor is so high but the poorest may hope to reach it."

CHESTER A. ARTHUR   *1881-1885*

"No higher proof could exist of the strength of popular government than the fact that, though the chosen of the people be struck down, his constitutional successor is peacefully installed without shock or strain."

GROVER CLEVELAND   *1885-1889—1893-1897*

"Our nation . . . lives in us—in our hearts and minds and consciences. . . . The land we live in seems to be strong and active. But how fares the land that lives in us?"

BENJAMIN HARRISON   *1889-1893*

"Our growth has not been limited to territory, population and aggregate wealth. . . The facilities for popular education have been vastly enlarged and more greatly diffused."

WILLIAM McKINLEY   *1897-1901*

"The mission of the United States is one of benevolent assimilation, substituting the mild sway of justice and right for arbitrary rule."

THEODORE ROOSEVELT   *1901-1909*

"Like all Americans, I like big things: big prairies, big forests and mountains, big wheatfields, railroads . . . and everything else. But no people ever yet benefited by riches if their prosperity corrupted their virtue."

WILLIAM HOWARD TAFT   *1909-1913*

"We have taken millions of foreigners into our civilization, but we have amalgamated them, and . . . we have made them all Americans. We have bred to a type."

WOODROW WILSON   *1913-1921*

"America . . . consists of all of us; and it can consist of all of us only as our spirits are banded together in a common enterprise. That common enterprise is the enterprise of liberty and justice and right."

Page Seventy Three

WARREN G. HARDING   *1921-1923*
"The motor car has become an indispensable instrument in our political, social and industrial life. There is begun a new era ..."

CALVIN COOLIDGE   *1923-1929*
"It would be folly to argue that the people cannot make political mistakes. They can and do make grave mistakes. But compared with the mistakes which have been made by every kind of autocracy they are unimportant."

HERBERT HOOVER   *1929-1933*
"We believe in equal opportunity for all, but we know that this includes the opportunity to rise to leadership, to be uncommon! The great human advances have not been brought about by mediocre men and women."

FRANKLIN D. ROOSEVELT   *1933-1945*
"This great Nation will endure as it has endured, will revive and will prosper... The only thing we have to fear is fear itself — which paralyzes needed efforts to convert retreat into advance."

HARRY S. TRUMAN   *1945-1953*
"We want to ... do the things in peace that we have been able to do in war. If we can put this tremendous machine of ours ... to work for peace, we can look forward to the greatest age in the history of mankind."

DWIGHT D. EISENHOWER   *1953-1961*
"What we call foreign affairs is no longer foreign affairs. It's a local affair. Whatever happens in Indonesia is important to Indiana. . . The world must learn to work together — or finally it will not work at all."

JOHN F. KENNEDY   *1961-1963*
"My fellow citizens of the world: ask not what America will do for you, but what together we can do for the freedom of man."

ON THE 185TH YEAR AFTER
PAUL REVERE'S RIDE
by
HENRY WADSWORTH LONGFELLOW *(last four verses)*

It was two by the village clock,
When he came to the bridge in Concord town.
He heard the bleating of the flock,
And the twitter of the birds among the trees,
And felt the breath of the morning breeze
Blowing over the meadows brown.
And one was safe and asleep in his bed
Who at the bridge would be first to fall,
Who that day would be lying dead,
Pierced by a British musket ball.

You know the rest. In the books you have read
How the British regulars fired and fled,—
How the farmers gave them ball for ball,
From behind each fence and farmyard-wall,
Chasing the red-coats down the lane,
Then crossing the fields to emerge again
Under the trees at the turn of the road,
And only pausing to fire and load.

So through the night rode Paul Revere;
And so through the night went his cry of alarm
To every Middlesex village and farm,—
A cry of defiance, and not of fear,—
A voice in the darkness, a knock at the door,
And a word that shall echo for evermore!

For, borne on the night-wind of the Past,
Through all our history, to the last,
In the hour of darkness, and peril, and need,
The people will waken to listen and hear
The hurrying hoof-beat of that steed,
And the midnight message of Paul Revere.

...*"think seriously of this ...*
fly to the place from whence you came"

*Few letters ever written have expressed, so cogently, the
feelings of the authors, as does this letter written in 1773,
to the Captain of a ship carrying tea from London to Philadelphia.*

To Capt. Ayres, of the Ship Polly, on a Voyage from
London to Philadelphia.

Sir,

We are informed that you have, imprudently, taken
charge of a quantity of tea; which has been sent out by the
India Company, *under the auspices of the Ministry,* as a trial
of *American* Virtue and Resolution.

Now, as your cargo, on your arrival here, will most assur-
edly bring you into hot water; and as you are perhaps a
stranger *to these Parts,* we have concluded to advise you of
the present situation of Affairs in *Philadelphia*—that, taking
time by the forelock, you may stop short in your dangerous
errand—secure your ship against the rafts of combustible
matter which may be set on Fire, and turned loose against
her: and more than all this, that you may preserve your own
person, from the pitch and feathers that are prepared for you.

In the first place, we must tell you, that the *Pennsylvan-
ians* are, *to a Man,* passionately fond of Freedom; the Birth-
right of *Americans;* and at all events are determined to enjoy
it.

That they sincerely believe, no power on the face of the
Earth has a right to tax them without their consent.

That in their opinion, the tea in your custody is designed
by the Ministry to enforce such a tax, which they will un-
doubtedly oppose; and in so doing, give you every possible
obstruction.

We are nominated to a very disagreeable, but necessary

service.–To our care are committed all offenders against the rights of *America;* and hapless is he, whose evil destiny has doomed him to suffer at our hands.

You are sent out on a diabolical service; and if you are so foolish and obstinate as to complete your voyage; by bringing your ship to anchor in this Port; you may run such a gauntlet, as will induce you, in your last moments, most heartily to curse those who have made you the dupe of their avarice and ambition.

What think you Captain, of a halter around your neck–ten Gallons of liquid tar decanted on your pate–with the feathers of a dozen wild geese laid over that to enliven your appearance?

Only think seriously of this–and fly to the place from whence you came–fly without hesitation–without the formality of a protest–and above all, Captain *Ayres* let us advise you to fly without the wild geese feathers.

Your Friends to serve

THE COMMITTEE as before subscribed.

Philadelphia, Nov. 27, 1773.

BEN FRANKLIN'S CELEBRATED LETTER
TO STRAHAN

As a sequel to the foregoing notices, we give Dr. Franklin's celebrated letter, written in the actual heat of the first outbreak.

Philadelphia, July 5, 1775.

Mr. STRAHAN,–You are a member of Parliament, and one of that majority which has doomed my country to destruction. You have begun to burn our towns, and murder our people. Look upon your hands! They are stained with the blood of your relations! You and I were long friends; you are now my enemy, and

I am, yours,   B. FRANKLIN.

JEFFERSON'S LETTER OF CREDIT TO LEWIS

[From original MS. in Bureau of Rolls — Jefferson Papers, series 1, vol. 9, doc. 94.][1]

WASHINGTON, U. S. OF AMERICA, July 4, 1803.

DEAR SIR : In the journey which you are about to undertake[2] for the discovery of the course and source of the Missouri, and of the most convenient water communication from thence to the Pacific ocean, your party being small, it is to be expected that you will encounter considerable dangers from the Indian inhabitants. should you escape those dangers and reach the Pacific ocean, you may find it imprudent to hazard a return the same way, and be forced to seek a passage round by sea, in such vessels as you may find on the Western coast. but you will be without money, without clothes, & other necessaries; as a sufficient supply cannot be carried with you from hence. your resource in that case can only be in the credit of the U. S. for which purpose I hereby authorise you to draw on the Secretaries of State, of the Treasury, of War & of the Navy of the U S. according as you may find your draughts will be most negociable, for the purpose of obtaining money or necessaries for yourself & your men; and I solemnly pledge the faith of the United States that these draughts shall be paid punctually at the date they are made payable. I also ask of the Consuls, agents, merchants & citizens of any nation with which we have intercourse or amity to furnish you with those supplies which your necessities may call for, assuring them of honorable and prompt retribution. and our own Consuls in foreign parts where you may happen to be, are hereby instructed & required to be aiding & assisting you in whatsoever may be necessary for procuring your return back to the United States. And to give more entire satisfaction & confidence to those who may be disposed to aid you, I Thomas Jefferson, President of the United States of America, have written this letter of general credit for you with my own hand, and signed it with my name.

TH: JEFFERSON

To Cap.t Meriwether Lewis.

HISTORIC FRANKLINISMS

"We must all hang together, else we shall all hang separately."
In reply to a remark of John Hancock, while the Declaration of Independence was being signed, July 4, 1776, that they must all hang together.

___

In a debate on taxation, in the Continental Congress, July, 1776, Mr. Lynch asked why slaves should be taxed more than sheep. "Sheep will never make insurrections," was Franklin's answer. Some one asked why the new boulevards of Paris were made so long and straight. "Bullets cannot turn corners," was the reply of Baron Haussmann, the Prefect of the Seine under Napoleon III.

___

Lord Howe spoke, in 1776, of England's need of American commerce and *men*. "Ay, my lord," assented Franklin: "we have in America a pretty considerable manufactory of men." When told that Lord Howe had taken Philadelphia, in 1777, "I beg your pardon, sir," retorted Franklin: "Philadelphia has taken Howe."

___

"Nothing is certain but death and taxes."
Franklin addressed a letter to M. Leroy, of the French Academy of Sciences, in 1789: "Our constitution is in actual operation; every thing appears to promise that it will last: but in this world nothing is certain but death and taxes."

— BENJAMIN FRANKLIN

It is a most unusual fact that George Washington passed away in the last hour, of the last day, of the last week, of the last month of the last year, of the eighteenth century.

LEWIS IN INDIAN DRESS, BY ST. MEMIN
From the original in possession of Mrs. Julia Clark Voorhis

THOMAS JEFFERSON'S TRIBUTE TO THE GREAT MERIWETHER LEWIS 'DISCOVERER OF THE NORTHWEST'

In planning for the leadership of this immortal expedition, Jefferson had, this time, no hesitancy in granting Captain Lewis's request to be entrusted with its direction. As Jefferson's private secretary, Lewis's qualifications for the chieftainship were now thoroughly known to the President. The tribute to him, found in Jefferson's Memoir, is worthy of reproduction here for more reasons than one:

I had now had opportunities of knowing him intimately. Of courage undaunted; possessing a firmness and perseverance of purpose which nothing but impossibilities could divert from its direction; careful as a father of those committed to his charge, yet steady in the maintenance of order and discipline; intimate with the Indian character, customs, and principles; habituated to the hunting life; guarded, by exact observation of the vegetables and animals of his own country, against losing time in the description of objects already possessed; honest, disinterested, liberal, of sound understanding, and a fidelity to truth so scrupulous that whatever he should report would be as certain as if seen by ourselves, —with all these qualifications, as if selected and implanted by nature in one body for this express purpose, I could have no hesitation in confiding the enterprise to him. To fill up the measure desired, he wanted nothing but a greater familiarity with the technical language of the natural sciences and readiness in the astronomical observations necessary for the geography of his route. To acquire these he repaired immediately to Philadelphia, and placed himself under the tutorage of the distinguished professors of that place, who, with a zeal and emulation enkindled by an ardent devotion to science, communicated to him freely the information requisite for the purpose of the journey. While attending, too, at Lancaster, the fabrication of the arms with which he chose that his men should be provided, he had the benefit of daily communication with Mr. Andrew Ellicot, whose experience in astronomical observation, and practice of it in the woods, enabled him to apprise Captain Lewis of the wants and difficulties he would encounter, and of the substitutes and resources offered by a woodland and uninhabited country.

"MY RACE IS NEARLY RUN,"
ANDREW JACKSON

The State of the Union
Was Troubled Then Also

We have now lived almost fifty years under the Constitution framed by the sages and patriots of the Revolution. The conflicts in which the nations of Europe were engaged during a great part of this period, the spirit in which they waged war against each other, and our intimate commercial connections with every part of the civilized world rendered it a time of much difficulty for the Government of the United States. We have had our seasons of peace and of war, with all the evils which precede or follow a state of hostility with powerful nations. We encountered these trials with our Constitution yet in its infancy, and under the disadvantages which a new and untried government must always feel when it is called upon to put forth its whole strength without the lights of experience to guide it or the weight of precedents to justify its measures. But we have passed triumphantly through all these difficulties. Our Constitution is no longer a doubtful experiment, and at the end of nearly half a century we find that it has preserved unimpaired the liberties of the people, secured the rights of property, and that our country has improved and is flourishing beyond any former example in the history of nations.

* * * * *

The necessity of watching with jealous anxiety for the preservation of the Union was earnestly pressed upon his fellow-citizens by the Father of his Country in his Farewell Address. He has there told us that "while experience shall not have demonstrated its impracticability, there will always be reason to distrust the patriotism of those who in any quarter may endeavor to weaken its bands"; and he has cautioned us in the strongest terms against the formation of parties on geographical discriminations, as one of the means which might disturb our Union and to which designing men would be likely to resort.

The lessons contained in this invaluable legacy of Washington to his countrymen should be cherished in the heart of every citizen to the latest generation; and perhaps at no period of time could they be more usefully remembered than at the present moment; for when we look upon the scenes that are passing around us and dwell upon the pages of his parting address, his paternal counsels would seem to be not merely the offspring of wisdom and foresight, but the voice of prophecy, foretelling events and warning us of the evil to come. Forty years have passed since this imperishable document was given to his countrymen. The Federal Constitution was then regarded by him as an experiment—and he so speaks of it in his Address—but an experiment upon the success of which the best hopes of his country depended; and we all know that he was prepared to lay down his life, if necessary, to secure to it a full and a fair trial. The trial has been made. It has succeeded beyond the produest hopes of those who framed it.

* * * * *

In presenting to you, my fellow-citizens, these parting counsels, I have brought before you the leading principles upon which I endeavored to administer the Government in the high office with which you twice honored me. Knowing that the path of freedom is continually beset by enemies who often assume the disguise of friends, I have devoted the last hours of my public life to warn you of the dangers. The progress of the United States under our free and happy institutions has surpassed the most sanguine hopes of the founders of the Republic. Our growth has been rapid beyond all former example in numbers, in wealth, in knowledge, and all the useful arts which contribute to the comforts and convenience of man, and from the earliest ages of history to the present day there never have been thirteen millions of people associated in one political body who enjoyed so much freedom and happiness as the people of these United States. You have no longer any cause to fear dan-

The people's government made for the people,
made by the people, and answerable to the people.
—DANIEL WEBSTER.

ger from abroad; your strength and power are well known throughout the civilized world, as well as the high and gallant bearing of your sons. It is from within, among yourselves—from cupidity, from corruption, from disappointed ambition and inordinate thirst for power—that factions will be formed and liberty endangered. It is against such designs, whatever disguise the actors may assume, that you have especially to guard yourselves. You have the highest of human trusts committed to your care. Providence has showered on this favored land blessings without number, and has chosen you as the guardians of freedom, to preserve it for the benefit of the human race. May He who holds in His hands the destinies of nations make you worthy of the favors He has bestowed and enable you, with pure hearts and pure hands and sleepless vigilance, to guard and defend to the end of time the great charge He has committed to your keeping.

My own race is nearly run; advanced age and failing health warn me that before long I must pass beyond the reach of human events and cease to feel the vicissitudes of human affairs. I thank God that my life has been spent in a land of liberty and that He has given me a heart to love my country with the affection of a son. And filled with gratitude for your constant and unwavering kindness, I bid you a last and affectionate farewell.

> *You are old Father Williams, the young man cried,*
> *The few locks which are left you are grey;*
> *You are hale, Father William, a hearty old man,*
> *Now tell me the reason, I pray.*
>
> *In the days of my youth, Father William replied,*
> *I remember'd that youth would fly fast,*
> *And abused not my health and my vigor at first,*
> *That I never might need them at last.*
> —ROBERT SOUTHEY, *The Old Man's Comforts.*

ANDREW JACKSON – BELOVED AUTOCRAT

From Life of ANDREW JACKSON –JAMES PARTON

"Yes, autocrat as he was, Andrew Jackson loved the people, the common people, the sons and daughters of toil, as truly as they loved him, and believed in them as they believed in him. He was in accord with his generation. He had a clear perception that the toiling millions are not a class in the community, but *are* the community. He knew and felt that government should exist only for the benefit of the governed; that the strong are strong only as they may aid the weak; that the rich are rightfully rich only that they may so combine and direct the labor of the poor as to make labor more profitable to the laborer. He did not comprehend these truths as they are demonstrated by Jefferson and Spencer, but he had an intuitive and instinctive perception of them. And in his most autocratic moments, he really thought that he was fighting the battle of the people and doing their will while baffling the purposes of their representatives. If he had been a man of knowledge as well as force, he would have taken the part of the people more effectually, and left to his successors an increased power of doing good, instead of better facilities for doing harm. He appears always to have meant well. But his ignorance of law, history, politics, science, of every thing which he who governs a country ought to know was extreme. Mr. Trist remembers hearing a member of the General's family say, that General Jackson did not believe the world was round. His ignorance was as a wall round about him—high, impenetrable. He was imprisoned in his ignorance, and sometimes raged round his little, dim inclosure like a tiger in his den."

ABRAHAM LINCOLN TELLS
OF HIS LIFE ON THE FRONTIER

"I was born February 12, 1809, in Hardin county, Kentucky. My parents were both born in Virginia, of undistinguished families—second families, perhaps I should say. My mother, who died in my tenth year, was of a family of the name of Hanks. . . . My paternal grandfather, Abraham Lincoln, emigrated from Rockingham county, Virginia, to Kentucky about 1781 or 1782, where, a year or two later, he was killed by the Indians, not in battle, but by stealth, when he was laboring to open a farm in the forest.

"My father (Thomas Lincoln) at the death of his father was but six years of age. By the early death of his father, and the very narrow circumstances of his mother, he was, even in childhood, a wandering, laboring boy, and grew up literally without education. He never did more in the way of writing than bunglingly to write his own name. . . . He removed from Kentucky to what is now Spencer county, Indiana, in my eighth year. . . . It was a wild region, with many bears and other animals still in the woods. . . . There were some schools, so-called, but no qualification was ever required of a teacher beyond 'readin', writin', and cipherin' to the rule of three.' If a straggler supposed to understand Latin happened to sojourn in the neighborhood he was looked upon as a wizard. . . . Of course, when I came of age I did not know much. Still, somehow, I could read, write, and cipher to the rule of three. But that was all. . . . The little advance I now have upon this store of education I have picked up from time to time under the pressure of necessity.

Whenever I hear anyone arguing for slavery,
I feel a strong impulse to see it tried on
him personally.
                                             —A. LINCOLN.

"I was raised to farm work ... till I was twenty-two. At twenty-one I came to Illinois,—Macon county. Then I got to New Salem, ... where I remained a year as a sort of clerk in a store. Then came the Black Hawk war; and I was elected captain of a volunteer company, a success that gave me more pleasure than any I have had since. I went into the campaign—was elated—ran for the Legislature the same year (1832), and was beaten—the only time I ever have been beaten by the people. The next, and three succeeding biennial elections, I was elected to the Legislature. I was not a candidate afterward. During the legislative period I had studied law and removed to Springfield to practice it. In 1846 I was elected to the lower house of Congress. Was not a candidate for re-election. From 1849 to 1854, inclusive, practised law more assiduously than ever before. Always a Whig in politics, and generally on the Whig electoral tickets, making active canvasses. I was losing interest in politics when the repeal of the Missouri Compromise aroused me again.

"If any personal description of me is thought desirable, it may be said that I am in height six feet four inches, nearly; lean in flesh, weighing on an average one hundred and eighty pounds; dark complexion, with coarse black hair and gray eyes. No other marks or brands recollected."

If the good people in their wisdom shall see fit to keep me in the background, I have been too familiar with disappointment to be much chagrined.

—A. LINCOLN, *When first a candidate to the Illinois legislature, 1832.*

BROTHER:
"Go To Work for the Best
Wages You Can Get"—A. Lincoln

"SPRINGFIELD, January 2, 1851.–Dear Brother: Your request for eighty dollars I do not think it best to comply with
now. At the various times I have helped you a little you
have said: 'We can get along very well now,' but in a short
time I find you in the same difficulty again. Now this can
only happen through some defect in you. What that defect
is I think I know. You are not lazy, and still you are an
idler. I doubt whether since I saw you you have done a
good, whole day's work in any one day. You do not very
much dislike to work, and still you do not work much,
merely because it does not seem to you you get enough
for it. This habit of uselessly wasting time is the whole
difficulty. It is vastly important to you, and still more to
your children, that you break the habit. . . .

"You are now in need of some money, and what I propose
is that you shall go to work, 'tooth and nail,' for somebody
who will give you money for it. Let father and your boys
take charge of your things at home, prepare for a crop and
make the crop, and you go to work for the best money
wages you can get, or in discharge of any debt you owe,
and, to secure you a fair reward for your labor, I promise
you that for every dollar you will get for your labor between
this and the 1st of May, either in money, or in your indebt-
edness, I will then give you one other dollar. By this, if you
hire yourself for ten dollars a month, from me you will get
ten dollars more, making twenty dollars. . . .

"In this I do not mean that you shall go off to St. Louis
or the lead mines in Missouri, or the gold mines in Cali-
fornia, but I mean for you to go at it for the best wages
you can get close to home in Coles county. If you will do
this you will soon be out of debt, and, what is better, you

will have acquired a habit which will keep you from getting in debt again. But if I should now clear you out of debt, next year you would be just as deep in debt as ever.

"You say you would almost give your place in Heaven for seventy or eighty dollars? Then you value your place in Heaven very cheap, for I am sure you can, with the offer I make, get the seventy or eighty dollars for four or five months' work.

"You say if I will lend you the money, you will deed me the land, and, if you don't pay the money back, you will deliver possession. Nonsense! If you cannot now live with the land, how will you then live without it?

"You have always been kind to me, and I do not mean to be unkind to you. On the contrary, if you but follow my advice, you will find it worth eighty times eighty dollars to you.

"Affectionately your brother,

"A. LINCOLN."

> And when with grief you see your brother stray
> Or in a night of error lose his way,
> Direct his wandering and restore the day . . .
> Leave to avenging Heaven his stubborn will,
> For, O, remember, he's your brother still.
>
> —SWIFT, *The Swain Tripe Club*

"A House Divided Against Itself Cannot Stand."

On June 16, 1858, the Illinois Republican convention named Lincoln as "first and only choice" for Senator. Lincoln, in acceptance, delivered his famous "House Divided" speech, attacking what seemed to him a conspiracy for the advancement of slavery. Friends who had seen the speech prior to its delivery had warned Lincoln that he took too strong a stand, and the speech did, in fact, mark Lincoln as a radical in some quarters. In this historic speech Lincoln said: "A house divided against itself cannot stand. I believe this government cannot endure, permanently, half *slave* and half *free*. I do not expect the Union to be *dissolved*—I don't expect the house to *fall* . . . but I do expect it will cease to be divided. It will become *all* one thing, or *all* the other."

From speech of Abraham Lincoln delivered at the Cooper Institute, New York City, Feb. 27, 1860: "Let us have faith that right makes might, and in that faith, let us, to the end, dare to do our duty as we undersand it."

Power tends to corrupt, and absolute power corrupts absolutely.
—LORD ACTON

LINCOLN'S ADVICE TO ATTORNEYS

from a 3-page holograph document by Abraham Lincoln *(from the Robert Todd Lincoln collection)*. Written about 1850.

"I am not an accomplished lawyer. I find quite as much material for a lecture in this point, wherein I have failed as on those wherein I have been modestly successful.

"The leading rule for the lawyer, as for the man of any other calling, is diligence. Leave nothing for tomorrow, which can be done today. Never let your correspondence fall behind. Whatever piece of business you have in hand before stopping, do all the better pertaining to it, which can then be done. When you bring a common lawsuit, if you have the facts for doing so, write the declaration at once. If a law point be involved, examine the book and note the authority you rely on for the declaration itself where you are sure to find it when wanted. The same of defenses and pleas.

"In business not likely to be litigation, ordinary circumstances, foreclosures, petitions and the like, make all examination and notes then and even draft orders and decrees in advance. This course has a large advantage; it avoids omissions and neglect, *saves* you labor when once done, performs the labor out of court when you *have* leisure, rather than in court, when you have not.

"Extemporaneous speaking should be practiced and cultivated. It is the lawyer's avenue to the public. However able and faithful he may be in other respects, people are slow to bring him business if he can not make a speech. And yet there is not a more fatal error to young lawyers, than relying too much on speechmaking. If anyone do to his powers of speaking, shall claim an exemption from knowing the law, his case is a failure in advance.

"Discourage litigation. Persuade your neighbors to compromise wherever you can. Point out to them how the nonsense winner is often the *real* loser in fees, expenses and waste of time. As a peacemaker, the lawyer has a superior opportunity of being a good man. There will still be business enough."

Lincoln comments on the close election which his party narrowly lost

". . . like a rejected lover
making merry at the wedding of his rival"

[Fragment of a speech of Abraham Lincoln at the Republican banquet in Chicago, December 10, 1856. The rest of this speech, if it was ever reported, is presumably no longer extant, as it is not published in any collection of Lincoln's speeches.]

GENTLEMEN: —We have another annual presidential message. Like a rejected lover making merry at the wedding of his rival, the President felicitates himself hugely over the late presidential election. He considers the result a signal triumph of good principles and good men, and a very pointed rebuke of bad ones. He says the people did it. He forgets that the "people," as he complacently calls only those who voted for Buchanan, are in a minority of the whole people by about four hundred thousand votes—one full tenth of all the votes. Remembering this, he might perceive that the "rebuke" may not be quite as durable as he seems to think—that the majority may not choose to remain permanently rebuked by that minority.

The President thinks the great body of us Fremonters, being ardently attached to liberty, in the abstract, were duped by a few wicked and designing men. There is a slight difference of opinion on this. We think he, being ardently attached to the hope of a second term, in the concrete, was duped by men who hate liberty every way. He is the cat's-paw. By much dragging of chestnuts from the fire for others to eat, his claws are burnt off to the gristle, and he is thrown aside as unfit for further use. As the fool said of King Lear, when his daughters had turned him out of doors, "He's a shelled peascod."

So far as the President charges us with a desire to "change the domestic institutions of existing States," and of "doing everything in our power to deprive the Constitution and the laws of moral authority," for the whole party on belief, and for myself on knowledge, I pronounce the charge an unmixed and unmitigated falsehood.

"IN THIS LIFE WE GET NOTHING SAVE BY EFFORT"

We do not admire the man of timid peace. We admire the man who embodies victorious effort; the man who never wrongs his neighbor; who is prompt to help a friend; but who has those virile qualities necessary to win in the stern strife of actual life. It is hard to fail; but it is worse never to have tried to succeed. In this life we get nothing save by effort. Freedom from effort in the present, merely means that there has been stored up effort in the past. A man can be freed from the necessity of work only by the fact that he or his fathers before him have worked to good purpose. If the freedom thus purchased is used aright, and the man still does actual work, though of a different kind, whether as a writer or a General, whether in the field of politics or in the field of exploration and adventure, he shows he deserves his good fortune. But if he treats this period of freedom from the need of actual labor as a period not of preparation but of mere enjoyment, he shows that he is simply a cumberer on the earth's surface; and he surely unfits himself to hold his own with his fellows if the need to do so should again arise. A mere life of ease is not in the end a satisfactory life, and above all it is a life which ultimately unfits those who follow it for serious work in the world.

—THEODORE ROOSEVELT

Our country, right or wrong. When right, to be kept right; when wrong to be put right.

—CARL SCHURZ *(October, 1899)*

General Lee's Last Words to His Army

Headquarters, Army of Northern Virginia,
April 10, 1865.

"After four years' of arduous service, marked by un-surpassed courage and fortitude, the Army of Northern Virginia has been compelled to yield to overwhelming numbers and resources. I need not tell the survivors of so many hard-fought battles, who have remained stead-fast to the last, that I have consented to this result from no distrust of them; but, feeling that valour and devotion could accomplish nothing that could compen-sate for the loss that would have attended the contin-uation of the contest, I have determined to avoid the useless sacrifice of those whose past services have en-deared them to their countrymen. By the terms of the agreement, officers and men can return to their homes and remain there until exchanged. You will take with you the satisfaction that proceeds from the conscious-ness of duty faithfully performed; and I earnestly pray that a merciful God will extend to you His blessing and protection. With an increasing admiration of your con-stancy and devotion to your country, and a grateful remembrance of your kind and generous consideration of myself, I bid you an affectionate farewell.

"R. E. LEE, GENERAL."

IMMORTAL WORDS BY IMMORTAL MEN

From a speech of Thomas Jefferson, President of the United States, delivered at his inauguration, March 4, 1801.

"Let us then, with courage and confidence, pursue our own federal and republican principles; our attachment to union and representative government. Kindly separated by nature and a wide ocean, from the exterminating havoc of one quarter of the globe; too high minded to endure the degradations of the others, possessing a chosen country, with room enough for our descendants to the thousandth and thousandth generation; entertaining a due sense of our equal right to the use of our own faculties, to the acquisitions of our own industry, to honor and confidence from our fellow citizens; resulting not from birth but from our actions and their sense of them; enlightened by a benign religion professed in deed and practised in various forms, yet all of them inculcating honesty, truth, temperance, gratitude and the love of man; acknowledging and adoring an overruling Providence, which, by all its dispensations, proves that it delights in the happiness of man hereafter; with all these blessings, what more is necessary to make us a happy and prosperous people?
"Still one thing more, fellow citizens, a wife and frugal government, which shall restrain man from injuring one another, shall leave them otherwise free to regulate their own pursuits of industry and improvement and shall not take from the mouth of labor the bread it has earned. This is the sum of good government; and this is necessary to close the circle of our felicities."

•   •   •

Last words of President Wilson's address, asking for a declaration of war, to Congress, April 2, 1917—

". . . the right is more precious than peace, and we shall fight for the things that we have always carried nearest our hearts— for democracy, for the right of those who submit to authority to have a voice in their own governments, for the rights and liberties of small nations, for a universal dominion of right by such a concert of free peoples as shall bring peace and safety to all nations and make the world itself at last free. To such a task, we can dedicate our lives and our fortunes, everything that we are and everything that we have, with the pride of those who know the day has come when America is privileged to spend her blood and her might for the principles that gave her birth and happiness and the peace which she has treasured. God helping her, she can do no other."

FROM THE TAFT MEMORIAL TOWER
WASHINGTON, D. C.

Liberty has been the key to
our progress in the past
and is the key to
our progress in the future.
If we can preserve liberty
in all its essentials;
There is no limit to the future
of the American People.
ROBERT A. TAFT

If we wish to make democracy
permanent in this country,
let us abide
by the fundamental principles
laid down in the Constitution.
Let us see that the
State is the servant
of its people and that the
people are not the servants
of the state.
ROBERT A. TAFT

You may tell me that these views are visionary, that the
destiny of this country is less exalted, that the American
people are less great than I think they are or ought to be. I
answer, ideals are like stars; you will not succeed in touching them with your hands. But like the seafaring man on
the desert of waters, you choose them as your guides, and
following them you will reach your destiny.
—CARL SCHURZ (April, 1859)

SIGH NO MORE, LADIES

SIGH no more, ladies, sigh no more,
    Men were deceivers ever;
One foot in sea, and one on shore;
    To one thing constant never.
        Then sigh not so,
        But let them go,
And be you blithe and bonny,
Converting all your sounds of woe
Into, Hey nonny, nonny!

Sing no more ditties, sing no mo
    Of dumps so dull and heavy:
The fraud of men was ever so,
    Since summer first was leavy.
        Then sigh not so,
        But let them go,
And be you blithe and bonny,
Converting all your sounds of woe
Into Hey nonny, nonny!

SHAKESPEARE (1564-1616).

Oh, let the clouds grow dark above,
    My heart is light below;
'Tis always summer when we love,
    However winds may blow;
And I'm as proud as any prince,
    All honors I disdain:
She says I am her rain beau since
    I kissed her in the rain.

    — SAMUEL MINTURN PECK
    A Kiss In The Rain

DELIA

Fair the face of orient day,
Fair the tints of op'ning rose;
But fairer still my Delia dawns,
More lovely far her beauty blows.

Sweet the lark's wild-warbled lay,
Sweet the tinkling rill to hear;
But, Delia, more delightful still,
Steal thine accents on mine ear.

The flower-enamour'd busy bee
The rosy banquet loves to sip;
Sweet the streamlet's limpid lapse
To the sun-brown'd Arab's lip.

But, Delia, on thy balmy lips
Let me, no vagrant insect, rove!
O let me steal one liquid kiss!
For oh! my soul is parch'd with love.

—ROBERT BURNS

THE KISS

"I SAW you take his kiss!" " 'Tis true."
    "O, modesty!" " 'Twas strictly kept:
He thought me asleep; at least, I knew
    He thought I thought he thought I slept."

—COVENTRY PATMORE (1823-1896)

READING

. . . We get no good
By being ungenerous, even to a book
And calculating profits . . . so much help
By so much reading. It is rather when
We gloriously forget ourselves and plunge
Soul-forward, headlong, into a book's profound,
Impassioned for its beauty and salt of truth —
'Tis then we get the right good from a book.

— ELIZABETH B. BROWNING
"Aurora Leigh"

A RIDDLE
(A BOOK)

I'm a strange contradiction; I'm new, and I'm
old,
I'm often in tatters, and oft decked with gold.
Though I never could read, yet lettered I'm
found;
Though blind, I enlighten; though loose, I am
bound,
I'm always in black, and I'm always in white;
I'm grave and I'm gay, I am heavy and light—
In form too I differ—I'm thick and I'm thin,
I've no flesh and no bones, yet I'm covered with
skin;
I've more points than the compass, more stops
than the flute;
I sing without voice, without speaking confute.
I'm English, I'm German, I'm French, and I'm
Dutch;
Some love me too fondly, some slight me too
much;
I often die soon, though I sometimes live ages,
And no monarch alive has so many pages.

—HANNAH MORE

ANY ONE WILL DO

A maiden once, of certain age,
To catch a husband did engage;
But, having passed the prime of life
In striving to become a wife
Without success, she thought it time
To mend the follies of her prime.

Departing from the usual course
Of paint and such like for resource,
With all her might this ancient maid
Beneath an oak-tree knelt and prayed;
Unconscious that a grave old owl
Was perched above—the mousing fowl!

"Oh, give! a husband give!" she cried,
"While yet I may become a bride;
Soon will my day of grace be o'er,
And then, like many maids before,
I'll die without an early love,
And none to meet me there above!

"Oh, 'tis a fate too hard to bear!
Then answer this my humble prayer,
And oh, a husband give to me!"
Just then the owl from out the tree,
In deep bass tones cried, "Who—who—who!"
"Who, Lord? And dost Thou ask me who?
Why, any one, good Lord, will do."

Anonymous

*Needles and Pins, needles and pins,
When a man marries his trouble begins.*

ADVICE TO A GIRL

NEVER love unless you can
Bear with all the faults of man:
Men sometimes will jealous be,
Though but little cause they see;
And hang the head as discontent,
And speak what straight they will repent.

Men that but one saint adore
Make a show of love to more;
Beauty must be scorned in none,
Though but truly served in one;
For what is courtship but disguise?
True hearts may have dissembling eyes.

Men, when their affairs require,
Must awhile themselves retire;
Sometimes hunt, and sometimes hawk,
And not ever sit and talk.
If these and such-like you can bear,
Then like, and love, and never fear!
                    —THOMAS CAMPION (1567-1620)

When he presented his "Essay on the Geometry of the Infinite" to Regent in 1727, Fontenelle remarked, "Here is a book which only eight men in France are capable of understanding, and the author is not one of that number."

There are three things I have always loved, and never understood—painting, music, and women.

She gave me one cold parting kiss upon my forehead, like a thaw-drop from the stone porch.
*   — CHARLES DICKENS — Bleak House*

It is seventy-five years since the death of Emily Dickinson

Like a faint, lingering echo of the vanishing past comes the memory of this New England poet, who typifies the life of a cultured woman of a different era, reared in the sequestered society of a New England college town; a woman who moved quietly and daintily through life, sheltered and protected from the strife and bustle of the busy world. She was born in 1830, at Amherst, Mass., and lived all her peaceful days and died there in the classic atmosphere of Amherst College, of which her father, Edward Dickinson, was treasurer.

The story of her life is singularly uneventful; she never traveled, and the interests of the town in which she lived revolved around the college, whose academic society was completely self-sufficient. Nevertheless Miss Dickinson evolved through her own intellect and imagination a philosophy of life broader and finer than many who have the advantages of travel and worldly experience. She frankly confessed her limitations in a little poem called:

CHARTLESS

I never saw a moor,
I never saw the sea;
Yet know I how the heather looks,
And what a wave must be.

Then she continues in a burst of sublime intuition:

I never spoke with God,
Nor visited in heaven;
Yet certain am I of the spot
As if the chart were given.

In another poem called "Parting" she expresses the wisdom gained in sorrow by each human being:

Parting is all we know of heaven,
And all we need of hell.

Miss Dickinson died at Amherst in 1886, but it was not until four years later that her poems and letters were published.

THE MYSTERY OF PAIN

Pain has an element of blank;
    It cannot recollect
When it began, or if there were
    A day when it was not.

It has no future but itself,
    Its infinite realms contain
Its past, enlightened to perceive
    New periods of pain.

"I TASTE A LIQUOR NEVER BREWED"

I taste a liquor never brewed
    From tankards scooped in pearl;
Not all the vats upon the Rhine
    Yield such an alcohol!

Inebriate of air am I,
    And debauchee of dew,
Reeling, through endless summer days,
    From inns of molten blue.

When landlords turn the drunken bee
    Out of the foxglove's door,
When butterflies renounce their drams,
    I shall but drink the more!

Till seraphs swing their snowy hats,
    And saints to windows run,
To see the little tippler
    Leaning against the sun!

Both from EMILY DICKINSON'S *Poems*

A BOOK

He ate and drank the precious words,
  His spirit grew robust;
He knew no more that he was poor,
  Nor that his frame was dust.
He danced along the dingy days,
  And this bequest of wings
Was but a book. What liberty
  A loosened spirit brings!

PROOF

That I did always love,
  I bring thee proof;
That till I loved
  I did not love enough.

That I shall love alway,
  I offer thee
That love is life,
  And life hath immortality.

This, dost thou doubt, sweet?
  Than have I
Nothing to show
  But Calvary.

"THE PEDIGREE OF HONEY"

The pedigree of honey
  Does not concern the bee;
A clover, any time, to him
  Is aristocracy.

from Poems by EMILY DICKINSON

INDIAN SUMMER

These are the days when birds come back,
   A very few, a bird or two,
To take a backward look.

These are the days when skies put on
   The old, old sophistries of June, —
A blue and gold mistake.

Oh, fraud that cannot cheat the bee,
   Almost thy plausibility,
Induces my belief,

Till ranks of seeds their witness bear,
   And softly through the altered air
Hurries a timid leaf!

Oh, sacrament of summer days,
   Oh, last communion in the haze,
Permit a child to join,

Thy sacred emblems to partake,
   Thy consecrated bread to break,
Taste thine immortal wine!

AUTUMN

The morns are meeker than they were,
   The nuts are getting brown;
The berry's cheek is plumper,
   The rose is out of town.

The maple wears a gayer scarf,
   The field a scarlet gown.
Lest I should be old-fashioned,
   I'll put a trinket on.

*Both from Poems—*EMILY DICKINSON

THE MOUNTAIN

The mountain sat upon the plain
   In his eternal chair,
His observation omnifold,
   His inquest everywhere.

The seasons prayed around his knees,
   Like children round a sire;
Grandfather of the days is he,
   Of dawn the ancestor.

A DAY

I'll tell you how the sun rose, –
   A ribbon at a time.
The steeples swam in amethyst,
   The news like squirrels ran.

The hills untied their bonnets,
   The bobolinks begun,
Then I said softly to myself,
   "That must have been the sun!"

But how he set, I know not.
   There seemed a purple stile
Which little yellow boys and girls
   Were climbing all the while.

Till when they reached the other side,
   A dominie in gray
Put gently up the evening bars,
   And led the flock away.

Both from Poems—EMILY DICKINSON

BECLOUDED

The sky is low, the clouds are mean,
  A traveling flake of snow
Across a barn or through a rut
  Debates if it will go.

A narrow wind complains all day
  How some one treated him;
Nature, like us, is sometimes caught
  Without her diadem.

"THERE'S A CERTAIN SLANT OF LIGHT"

There's a certain slant of light,
  On winter afternoons,
That oppresses, like the weight
  Of cathedral tunes.

Heavenly hurt it gives us;
  We can find no scar,
But internal difference
  Where the meanings are.

None may teach it anything,
  'Tis the seal, despair, –
An imperial affliction
  Sent us of the air.

When it comes, the landscape listens,
  Shadows hold their breath;
When it goes, 'tis like the distance
  On the look of death.

from Poems by EMILY DICKINSON

GIFTS RETURNED

"You must give back," her mother said,
To a poor sobbing little maid,
"All the young man has given you,
Hard as it now may seem to do."
" 'Tis done already, mother dear!"
Said the sweet girl, "So never fear."
    Mother. Are you quite certain? Come, recount
(There was not much) the whole amount.
    Girl. The locket; the kid gloves.
    Mother.   Go on.
    Girl. Of the kid gloves I found but one.
    Mother. Never mind that. What else? Proceed.
You gave back all his trash?
    Girl.   Indeed.
    Mother. And was there nothing you would save?
    Girl. Everything I could give I gave.
    Mother. To the last tittle?
    Girl.   Even to that.
    Mother. Freely?
    Girl.   My heart went pit-a-pat
At giving up . . . ah me! ah me!
I cry so I can hardly see . . .
All the fond looks and words that past,
And all the kisses, to the last.

              WALTER SAVAGE LANDOR

Men, dying, make their wills, but wives
   Escape a work so sad;
Why should they make what all their lives
   The gentle dames have had?
            JOHN GODFREY SAXE

A BIT OF GELETT
BURGESS AT HIS BEST

I never saw a Purple Cow
I never hope to see one,
But I can tell you anyhow,
I'd rather see than be one.

Ah, yes, I wrote the "Purple Cow"—
I'm Sorry, now, I wrote it;
But I can tell you Anyhow
I'll Kill you if you Quote it!

AUTOMATIC ENGLISH

Said a miser who sordidly mised,
"My gold I have always despised;
I have stinged till I'm stingy,
And dinged till I'm dingy,
But it's really the practice I've prized!"

OR THIS –

There was an old man whom they called
    "weather-wise,"
For his prophecies ALWAYS came true,
If the day was so hot that it sun-struck
    the flies,
And he said it would snow, then it snew!

– GELETT BURGESS

I wish that my Room had a Floor!
I don't so much care for a Door,
    But this crawling around
    Without touching the Ground
Is getting to be quite a Bore!

I picked some Leaves from off a Tree,
    And then I nearly Fainted:
    For somehow it Astonished me
To find they'd All been Painted!

The Sun is Low, to say the Lease,
    Although it is well-Red;
Yet, since it rises in the Yeast,
    It should be better Bred.

Sunk in a leafy well, I lie
    And dreaming; gaze into the sky
Far up above the tree tops there;
    A lark swims through the vacant air.

I offer you my sincerest thanks, Mr. Caligraph. I will endeavor to place your advice into immediate execution forthwith. Allow me, Mr. Faber, to tender to yourself this little bijou of my own as a testimonial as a token of my esteem:

ALTHOUGH I'M YOUR TOOL,

I'll Be Nobody's Fool; I'll Be Firm if I AM a Utensil.
Do you see my point clear? – I must draw the line
    here,–
For I will not be Lead, Said the Pencil.

"Bessie had neatly hooked her game—A hundred fifty pounder"!

One morning when Spring was in her teens—
    A morn to a poet's wishing,
All tinted in delicate pinks and greens—
    Miss Bessie and I went fishing.

I in my rough and easy clothes,
    With my face at the sun-tan's mercy;
She with her hat tipped down to her nose,
    And her nose tipped—*vice versa.*

I with my rod, my reel, and my hooks,
    And a hamper for lunching recesses;
She with the bait of her comely looks,
    And the seine of her golden tresses.

So we sat us down on the sunny dike,
    Where the white pond-lilies teeter,
And I went to fishing like quaint old Ike,
    And she like Simon Peter.

All the noon I lay in the light of her eyes,
    And dreamily watched and waited,
But the fish were cunning and would not rise,
    And the baiter alone was baited.

And when the time of departure came,
    My bag hung flat as a flounder;
But Bessie had neatly hooked her game—
    A hundred-and-fifty-pounder.

                   ANONYMOUS

*Then come, my friend, forget your foes, and
    leave your fears behind,
And wander forth to try your luck, with
    cheerful quiet mind.*

      —HENRY VAN DYKE, *The Angler's Reveille.*

LOVE IN A COTTAGE

They may talk of love in a cottage,
  And bowers of trellised vine—
Of nature bewitchingly simple,
  And milkmaids half divine;
They may talk of the pleasure of sleeping
  In the shade of a spreading tree,
And a walk in the fields at morning,
  By the side of a footstep free!

But give me a sly flirtation
  By the light of a chandelier—
With music to play in the pauses,
  And nobody very near;
Or a seat on a silken sofa,
  With a glass of pure old wine,
And mamma too blind to discover
  The small white hand in mine.

Your love in a cottage is hungry,
  Your vine is a nest for flies—
Your milkmaid shocks the Graces,
  And simplicity talks of pies!
You lie down to your shady slumber
  And wake with a bug in your ear,
And your damsel that walks in the morning
  Is shod like a mountaineer.

True love is at home on a carpet,
  And mightily likes his ease—
And true love has an eye for a dinner,
  And starves beneath shady trees.
His wing is the fan of a lady,
  His foot's an invisible thing,
And his arrow is tipp'd with a jewel
  And shot from a silver string.
                    NATHANIEL PARKER WILLIS

SALAD

O cool in the summer is salad,
  And warm in the winter is love;
And a poet shall sing you a ballad
  Delicious thereon and thereof.
A singer am I, if no sinner,
  My muse has a marvelous wing,
And I willingly worship at dinner
    The Sirens of Spring.

Take endive—like love it is bitter,
  Take beet—for like love it is red;
Crisp leaf of the lettuce shall glitter,
  And cress from the rivulet's bed;
Anchovies, foam-born, like the lady
  Whose beauty has maddened this bard;
And olives, from groves that are shady;
    And eggs—boil 'em hard.
                        Mortimer Collins

  Conversation is but carving:
  Give no more to every guest
  Than he's able to digest;
  Give him always of the prime,
  And but little at a time;
  Give to all but just enough,
  Let them neither starve nor stuff
  And that each may have his due,
  Let your neighbor carve for you.

                        —Sir Walter Scott

Yet shall you have, to rectify your palate,
an olive, capers, or some better salad
ushering the mutton; with a short-legged hen,
If we can get her, full of eggs, and then,
Lemons, and wine for sauce: to these a coney
Is not to be despaired of for our money;
And though fowl now be scarce, yet there
    are clerks,
The sky not falling, think we may have larks.
                        —Ben Johnson, Epigrams

row old along
with me, the
st is yet to be...

A BACKWARD LOOK

by
JAMES WHITCOMB RILEY

As I sat smoking, alone, yesterday,
  And lazily leaning back in my chair,
Enjoying myself in a general way—
Allowing my thoughts a holiday
  From weariness, toil and care,—
My fancies—doubtless, for ventilation—
  Left ajar the gates of my mind,—
And Memory, seeing the situation,
  Slipped out in street of "Auld Lang Syne."

Wandering ever with tireless feet
  Through scenes of silence, and jubilee
Of long-hushed voices; and faces sweet
Were thronging the shadowy side of the street
  As far as the eye could see;
Dreaming again, in anticipation,
  The same old dreams of our boyhood's days
That never come true, from the vague sensation
  Of walking asleep in the world's strange ways.

Away to the house where I was born!
  And there was the selfsame clock that ticked
From the close of dusk to the burst of morn,
When life-warm hands plucked the golden corn
  And helped when the apples were picked.
And the "chany-dog" on the mantel-shelf,
  With the gilded collar and yellow eyes,
Looked just as at first, when I hugged myself
  Sound asleep with the dear surprise.

And down to the swing in the locust tree,
  Where the grass was worn from the trampled ground,
And where "Eck" Skinner, "Old" Carr, and three
Or four such other boys used to be
  Doin' "sky-scrapers," or "whirlin' round:"
And again Bob climbed for the bluebird's nest,
  And again "had shows" in the buggy-shed
Of Guymon's barn, where still, unguessed,
  The old ghosts romp through the best days dead!

And again I gazed from the old school-room
    With a wistful look of a long June day,
When on my cheek was the hectic bloom
Caught of Mischief, as I presume—
    He had such a "partial" way,
It seemed, toward me.—And again I thought
    Of a probable likelihood to be
Kept in after school—for a girl was caught
    Catching a note from me.

And down through the woods to the swimming-hole—
    Where the big, white, hollow, old sycamore grows,—
And we never cared when the water was cold,
And always "ducked" the boy that told
    On the fellow that tied the clothes.—
When life went so like a dreamy rhyme,
    That it seems to me now that then
The world was having a jollier time
    Than it ever will have again.

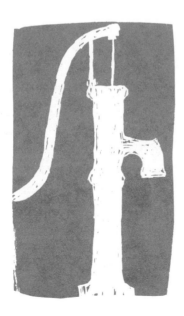

SIZES OF TYPE

From the AMERICAN LEGION MAGAZINE

The more our need to read increases,
The more the size of type decreases.
When we are young and have good sight,
We've primer type that's sharp and bright.

As time goes on and vision fades,
We must resort to optic aids;
And even so, with hope that's wary
We creep up on the dictionary.

When we grow old and eyesight fails us,
There's little help for that which ails us.
But still we must, by hook or crook,
Contrive to read the telephone book.

—BETTY SHAVER

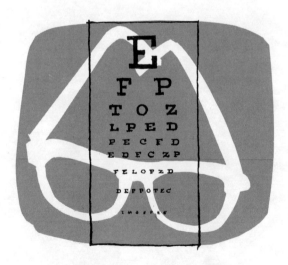

AN OLD MAN'S THOUGHT OF SCHOOL

by WALT WHITMAN

(Recited for the inauguration of a New Public School,
Camden, New Jersey, October 31, 1874)
Published in "Two Rivulets," 1876

An old man's thought of School;
An old man, gathering youthful memories and blooms,
    that youth itself cannot.

Now only do I know you!
O fair auroral skies! O morning dew upon the grass!

And these I see – these sparkling eyes,
These stores of mystic meaning – these young lives,
Building, equipping, like a fleet of ships – immortal ships!
Soon to sail out over the measureless seas,
On the Soul's voyage.

Only a lot of boys and girls?
Only the tiresome spelling, writing, ciphering classes?
Only a Public School?

Ah more – infinitely more;
(As George Fox rais'd his warning cry, "Is it this pile of
    brick and mortar – these dead floors, windows, rails –
    you call the church?
Why this is not the church at all – the Church is living,
    ever living Souls.")

And you, America,
Cast you the real reckoning for your present?
The lights and shadows of your future – good or evil?
To girlhood, boyhood look – the Teacher and the School.

NO TIME LIKE THE OLD TIME
by
OLIVER WENDELL HOLMES

There is no time like the old time, when
    you and I were young,
When the buds of April blossomed, and
    the birds of spring-time sung!
The garden's brightest glories by summer
    suns are nursed,
Buth oh, the sweet, sweet violets, the
    flowers that opened first!

There is no place like the old place, where
    you and I were born,
Where we lifted first our eyelids on the
    splendors of the morn
From the milk-white breast that warmed
    us, from the clinging arms that bore,
Where the dear eyes glistened o'er us that
    will look on us no more!

There is no friend like the old friend, who
    has shared our morning days,
No greeting like his welcome, no homage
    like his praise:
Fame is the scentless sunflower, with
    gaudy crown of gold;
But friendship is the breathing rose, with
    sweets in every fold.

There is no love like the old love, that we
    courted in our pride;
Though our leaves are falling, falling, and
    we're fading side by side,
There are blossoms all around us with the
    colors of our dawn,
And we live in borrowed sunshine when
    the day-star is withdrawn.

There are no times like the old times,—
  they shall never be forgot!
There is no place like the old place,—
  keep green the dear old spot!
There are no friends like our old friends,
  — may Heaven prolong their lives!
There are no loves like our old loves —
God bless our loving wives!

TIME LONG PAST
by PERCY B. SHELLEY

I
Like the ghost of a dear friend dead
  Is Time long past
A tone which is now forever fled,
A hope which is now forever past,
A love so sweet it could not last,
  Was Time long past.

II
There were sweet dreams in the night
  Of Time long past.
And, was it sadness or delight,
Each day a shadow onward cast
Which made us wish it yet might last —
  That Time long past.

III
There is regret, almost remorse,
  For Time long past.
'T is like a child's beloved corse
A father watches, till at last
Beauty is like remembrance cast
  From Time long past.

REMEMBER

Remember me when I am gone away,
   Gone far away into the silent land;
   When you can no more hold me by the hand,
Nor I half turn to go, yet turning stay.
Remember me when no more day by day
   You tell me of our future that you plann'd;
   Only remember me; you understand
It will be late to counsel then or pray.
Yet if you should forget me for a while
   And afterwards remember, do not grieve;
   For if the darkness and corruption leave
A vestige of the thoughts that once I had,
Better by far you should forget and smile
   Than that you should remember and be sad.

            — CHRISTINA GEORGINA ROSSETTI

WHEN YOU ARE OLD

When you are old and gray and full of sleep
   And, nodding by the fire, take down this book
   And slowly read, and dream of the soft look
Your eyes had once, and of their shadows deep;

How many loved your moments of glad grace
   And loved your beauty with love false or true;
   But one man loved the pilgrim soul in you,
And loved the sorrows of your changing face.

And bending down beside the glowing bars,
   Murmur, a little sadly, how love fled
   And paced upon the mountains overhead,
And hid his face amid a crowd of stars.

            —WILLIAM BUTLER YEATS

RESOLUTIONS WHEN I COME TO BE OLD

Written in 1699

Not to marry a young woman.

Not to keep young company, unless they desire it.

Not to be peevish, or morose, or suspicious.

Not to scorn present ways, or wits, or fashions, or men, or war, etc.

Not to be fond of children.

Not to tell the same story over and over to the same people.

Not to be covetous.

Not to neglect decency or cleanliness, for fear of falling into nastiness.

Not to be over severe with young people, but give allowances for their youthful follies and weaknesses.

Not to be influenced by, or give ear to, knavish tattling servants, or others.

Not to be too free of advice, or trouble any but those who desire it.

To desire some good friend to inform me which of these resolutions I break or neglect, and wherein, and reform accordingly.

Not to talk much, nor of myself.

Not to boast of my former beauty, or strength, or favor with ladies, etc.

Not to hearken to flatteries, nor conceive I can be beloved by a young woman; *et eos qui haereditatem captant, odisse ac vitare.*

Not to be positive or opinionative.

Not to set for observing all these rules, for fear I should observe none.

KUBLA KHAN

In Xanadu did Kubla Khan
A stately pleasure-dome decree:
Where Alph, the sacred river, ran
Through caverns measureless to man,
Down to a sunless sea.
So twice five miles of fertile ground
With walls and towers were girdled round:
And there were gardens bright with sinuous rills
Where blossomed many an incense-bearing tree;
And here were forests ancient as the hills,
Enfolding sunny spots of greenery.

— SAMUEL TAYLOR COLERIDGE

ANNABEL LEE

It was many and many a year ago,
In a kingdom by the sea,
That a maiden there lived, whom you may know
By the name of Annabel Lee;
And this maiden she lived with no other thought
Than to love and be loved by me.

I was a child, and *she* was a child,
In this kingdom by the sea;
But we loved with a love that was more than love,
I and my Annabel Lee,—
With a love that the winged seraphs of heaven
Coveted her and me.

—EDGAR ALLAN POE

Talent, lying in the understanding, is often inherited; genius, being the action of reason and imagination, rarely or never.

RECESSIONAL

God of our fathers, known of old —
Lord of our far-flung battle-line —
Beneath Whose awful Hand we hold
Dominion over palm and pine —
Lord God of Hosts, be with us yet,
Lest we forget — lest we forget!

— RUDYARD KIPLING

NOT ALL THREE

I turned to speak to God
About the world's despair;
But to make bad matters worse
I found God wasn't there.

God turned to speak to me
(Don't anybody laugh)
God found I wasn't there—
At least not over half.

God and the world we worship still together,
Draw not our laws to Him, but His to ours;
Untrue to both, so prosperous in neither,
The imperfect will brings forth but barren flowers!
Unwise as all distracted interests be,
Strangers to God, fools in humanity:
Too good for great things, and too great for good,
While still *"I dare not"* waits upon *"I would."*

— COLERIDGE

If ye do not hope, ye will not find: for in despairing, ye block up the mine at its mouth, ye extinguish the torch, even when ye are already in the shaft.

HOME-THOUGHTS FROM ABROAD

O, to be in England
Now that April's there,
And whoever wakes in England
Sees, some morning, unaware,
That the lowest boughs and the brushwood sheaf
Round the elm-tree bole are in tiny leaf,
While the chaffinch sings on the orchard bough
In England – now!

And after April, when May follows,
And the whitethroat builds, and all the swallows!
Hark, where my blossom'd pear-tree in the hedge
Leans to the field and scatters on the clover
Blossoms and dewdrops—at the bent spray's edge—
That's the wise thrush; he sings each song twice over,
Lest you should think he never could recapture
The first fine careless rapture!
And though the fields look rough with hoary dew,
All will be gay when noontide wakes anew
The buttercups, the little children's dower
—Far brighter than this gaudy melon-flower!

—ROBERT BROWNING

TWO HEAVENS

For there are two heavens, sweet,
    Both made of love,— one, inconceivable
Ev'n by the other, so divine it is;
The other, far on this side of the stars,
By men called home.
                    — LEIGH HUNT

GRIN

by ROBERT W. SERVICE
from the Spell of the Yukon and other verses
BARSE *and* HOPKINS

If you're up against a bruiser and you're getting knocked about –
          Grin.
If you're feeling pretty groggy, and you're
licked beyond a doubt –
          Grin.
Don't let him see you're funking, let him know
with every clout,
Though your face is battered to a pulp, your
blooming heart is stout;
Just stand upon your pins until the beggar
knocks you out –
          And grin.
This life's a bally battle, and the same advice
holds true
          Of grin.
If you're up against it badly, then it's only one
on you,
          So grin.
If the future's black as thunder, don't let people
see you're blue;
Just cultivate a cast-iron smile of joy the whole
day through;
If they call you "Little Sunshine," wish that
they'd no troubles, too –
          You may – grin.
Rise up in the morning with the will that,
smooth or rough,
          You'll grin.
Sink to sleep at midnight, and although you're
feeling tough,
          Yet grin.

There's nothing gained by whining, and you're
    not that kind of stuff;
You're a fighter from away back, and you *won't*
    take a rebuff;
Your trouble is that you don't know when you
    have had enough –
                Don't give in.
If Fate should down you, just get up and take
    another cuff;
You may bank on it that there is no philosophy
    like bluff,
                And grin.

GET THE JOB DONE!

There are two kinds of persons in the world: those who think first of difficulties, and those who think first of the importance of accomplishment in spite of difficulties. If a thing ought to be done, the presence of severe obstacles to its doing is only a further reason for bringing it to pass. Yet the trait of instantly showing why a thing cannot be done is keeping down more young men, and older men too, in business than any other factor in their lives. Anybody can point out difficulties; it calls for brain and courage to look beyond difficulties to the end. If you want to stay just where you are in the procession, or fall steadily behind, give obstacles a first place in your life. If you want to move out from the crowd, and count for something more than "average," let every obstacle be welcomed as a fresh incentive to action.

Difficulty is only a word indicating the degree of strength requisite for accomplishing particular objects; a mere notice of the necessity for exertion.

Great men rejoice in adversity
just as brave soldiers triumph in war.
                    —SENECA

MARK TWAIN TAKES A LESSON IN THE MANLY ART

WE MAY HAVE SAID some harsh things of Mark Twain, but now we take them all back. We feel like weeping for him—yea, we would fall on his breast and mingle our tears with his. But those manly shirt front of his air now a bloody one, and his nose is swollen to such an extent that to fall on his breast would be an utter impossibility.

Yesterday, he brought back all our things and promised us that he intended hereafter to lead a virtuous life. This was in the forenoon; in the afternoon he commenced the career of virtue he had marked out for himself and took a first lesson in boxing. Once he had the big gloves on, he imagined that he weighed a ton and could whip his weight in Greek-fire. He waded into a professor of the "manly art" like one of Howlan's rotary batteries, and the professor, in a playful way he has, when he wants to take the conceit out of forward pupils, let one fly straight out from the shoulder and "busted" Mr. Twain in the "snoot," sending him reeling—not exactly to grass, but across a bench—with two bountiful streams of "claret" spouting from his nostrils. At first his nose was smashed out till it covered nearly the whole of his face and looked like a large piece of tripe, but it was finally scraped into some resemblance of a nose, when he rushed away for surgical advice. Pools of gore covered the floor of the Club Room where he fought, and he left a bloody trail for half a mile through the city. It is estimated that he lost several hogsheads of blood in all. He procured a lot of sugar of lead and other cooling lotions and spent the balance of the day in applying them with towels and sponges.

After dark, he ventured forth with his nose swollen to the size of several junk bottles—a vast, inflamed and pulpy old snoot—to get advice about having it amputated. None of his friends recognize him now, and he spends his time in solitude, contemplating his ponderous vermillion smeller in a two-bit mirror, which he bought for that purpose. We cannot comfort him, for we know his nose will never be a nose again. It always was somewhat lopsided; now it is a perfect lump of blubber. Since the above was in type, the doctors have decided to amputate poor Mark Twain's smeller. A new one is to be made for him of a quarter of veal.

CASEY AT THE BAT

This classic was first recited by the author, Ernest Lawrence Thayer, Harvard '85, at the Harvard University class dinner in 1895. It was first printed in 1900 in answer to classmates' demands for it.

It looked extremely rocky for the Mudville nine that day,
The score stood four to six with but an inning left to play,
And so, when Cooney died at first, and Burrows did the same,
A pallor wreathed the features of the patrons of the game.

A straggling few got up to go, leaving there the rest,
With that hope which springs eternal within the human breast.
For they thought if only Casey could get a whack at that,
They'd put up even money with Casey at the bat.
But Flynn preceded Casey, and likewise so did Blake,
And the former was a pudding and the latter was a fake;
So on that striken multitude a death-like silence sat,
For there seemed but little chance of Casey's getting to the bat.
But Flynn let drive a single to the wonderment of all,
And the much despised Blakey tore the cover off the ball,
And when the dust had lifted and they saw what had occurred,
There was Blakey safe on second, and Flynn a-hugging third.
Then from the gladdened multitude went up a joyous yell,
It bounded from the mountain top and rattled in the dell,
It struck upon the hillside, and rebounded on the flat,
For Casey, mighty Casey, was advancing to the bat.
There was ease in Casey's manner as he stepped into his place,

There was pride in Casey's bearing and a smile on
    Casey's face,
And when responding to the cheers he lightly doffed his
    hat.
No stranger in the crowd could doubt, 'twas Casey at
    the bat.
Ten thousand eyes were on him as he rubbed his hands
    with dirt,
Five thousand tongues applauded as he wiped them on
    his shirt;
And while the writhing pitcher ground the ball into his
    hip—
Defiance gleamed from Casey's eye — a sneer curled
    Casey's lip.
And now the leather-covered sphere came hurtling
    through the air,
And Casey stood a-watching it in haughty grandeur
    there;
Close by the sturdy batsman the ball unheeded sped—
"That hain't my style," said Casey—"Strike one," the
    Umpire said.
From the bleachers black with people there rose a sullen
    roar,
Like the beating of the storm waves on a stern and
    distant shore,
"Kill him! kill the Umpire!" shouted some one from the
    stand—
And it's likely they'd have done it had not Casey raised
    his hand.
With a smile of Christian charity great Casey's visage
    shone,
He stilled the rising tumult and he bade the game go on;
He signalled to the pitcher and again the spheroid flew,
But Casey still ignored it and the Umpire said "Strike
    two."

> Sport begets tumultuous strife and wrath,
> and wrath begets fierce quarrels and war
> to the death.
> —HORACE, *Epistles.*

"Fraud!" yelled the maddened thousands, and the echo
answered "Fraud,"
But one scornful look from Casey and the audience was
awed;
They saw his face grow stern and cold; they saw his
muscles strain,
And they knew that Casey would not let that ball go by
again.
The sneer is gone from Casey's lip; his teeth are
clinched with hate,
He pounds with cruel violence his bat upon the plate;
And now the pitcher holds the ball, and now he lets it go,
And now the air is shattered by the force of Casey's
blow.
Oh! somewhere in this favored land the sun is shining
bright,
The band is playing somewhere, and somewhere hearts
are light,
And somewhere men are laughing, and somewhere
children shout;
But there is no joy in Mudville – mighty Casey has
"Struck Out."

No game was ever yet worth a rap
For a rational man to play,
Into which no accident, no mishap,
Could possibly find its way.

—A. L. GORDON, *Ye Weary Wayfarer.*

—A baseball fan standing in line to get into the
season opener between San Francisco and Pitts-
burgh in Candlestick park turned to his wife and
said:

"I wish I had brought the piano."
His wife, amazed, asked, "Why?"
"Because I left the tickets on it."

THE SOCIETY UPON THE STANISLAUS

I reside at Table Mountain, and my name is Truthful
    James;
I am not up to small deceit, or any sinful games;
And I'll tell in simple language what I know about the row
That broke up our Society upon the Stanislow.

But first I would remark, that it is not a proper plan
For any scientific gent to whale his fellow man,
And, if a member don't agree with his peculiar whim,
To lay for that same member for to "put a head" on him.

Now, nothing could be finer or more beautiful to see
Than the first six months' proceedings of that same
    society,
Till Brown of Calaveras brought a lot of fossil bones
That he found within a tunnel near the tenement of Jones.

Then Brown he read a paper, and he reconstructed there,
From those same bones, an animal that was extremely rare,
And Jones then asked the chair for a suspension of the
    rules,
Till he could prove that those same bones was one of his
    lost mules.

Then Brown he smiled a bitter smile, and said he was at
    fault;
It seemed he had been trespassing on Jones's family vault:
He was a most sarcastic man, this quiet Mr. Brown,
And on several occasions he had cleaned out the town.

Now, I hold it is not decent for a scientific gent
To say another is an ass—at least, to all intent:
Nor should the individual who happens to be meant
Reply by heaving rocks at him to any great extent.

Then Abner Dean of Angel's raised a point of order—when
A chunk of old red sandstone took him in the abdomen,
And he smiled a kind of sickly smile, and curled up on the
    floor,
And the subsequent proceedings interested him no more.

For, in less time than I write it, every member did engage
In a warfare with the remnants of a palaeozoic age;
And the way they heaved those fossils in their anger was
    a sin,
Till the skull of an old mammoth caved the head of
    Thompson in.

And this is all I have to say of these improper games,
For I live at Table Mountain, and my name is Truthful
    James;
And I've told in simple language what I know about the
    row
That broke up our Society upon the Stanislow.

Bret Harte

A WAIL

Rough Wind! that moanest loud
    Grief too sad for son,—
Wild Wind, when sullen cloud
    Knells all the night long!
Sad Storm, whose tears are vain!
Bare Woods, whose branches strain!
Deep Caves! and dreary Main!
    Wail for the world's wrong!

—JOHN KEATS

An Old Friend Can Never Be Found

and nature has provided that he cannot easily be lost

As people grow older friends and associates of
youth are apt to be more appreciated, and old
relations are oftentimes resumed that have been
suffered to languish for many years.

———

These links with the past form a chain that,
next to the ties of blood, forms one of the strongest relations of social life.

———

Esteem of great powers, or amiable qualities newly
discovered, may embroider a day or week, but a friendship of twenty years is interwoven with the texture
of life. A friend may be found and lost, but an **old
friend** never can be found, and nature has provided
that he cannot **easily** be lost.

— SAMUEL JOHNSON

———

An old friendship is like an old piece of china. It
is precious only just so long as it is perfect. Once it
is broken, no matter how cleverly you mend it, it is
good for nothing but to put on a shelf in a corner
where it won't be too closely looked at.

—AMELIA B. EDWARDS

———

One cannot be a friend without having one.

—A. S. HARDY

———

Times and places new we know,
Faces fresh and seasons strange,
But the friends of long ago
Do not change.

—ANDREW LANG

Prayer of the Salesman

God grant me the *will* to do my job—to make
my calls, to demonstrate my product,

Grant me the *humility* to accept rebuff with
grace; discourtesy with a grin; disappointment
with resolve—

Grant me the *courage* to face all obstacles, competitive
or otherwise, with determination and grit,

Grant me *loyalty* to my family, my company, my product
and my associates.

Grant me *enthusiasm* that I may impart this to my
prospect,

Grant me *stability* so that I may remain true to
myself in time of success—

Grant me *vision* that I may conserve the profit of
today's sale against the expense of tomorrow's
failure,

And, God, of course, above all grant me the favor of
my prospect's signature on the dotted line.

*Religion is the dominion of the soul. It is the
hope of life, the anchor of safety, the deliver-
ance of the soul.*
— NAPOLEON I

Napoleon was indeed a very great man, but he was
also a very great actor.
— DUKE OF WELLINGTON

TO PROSPER IN YOUR WORK— SERVE MORE PEOPLE BETTER

From an address by HUGHSTON M. MCBAIN,
Former Chairman, Marshall Field & Company

Superficial observers think because businessmen have money, or capitalists furnish money, that they are supreme. On the contrary, they are bound to obey unconditionally the "consumer captain's" orders. They cannot determine for long what to produce, how many to produce, or selling prices—the consumers do that. Every businessman knows that if he does not obey the orders of the public, if he does not serve the public by manufacturing what it likes, or offers goods and services for prices it will pay, he will suffer losses, eventually go bankrupt, and be completely removed from the scene. Other men who did better in satisfying the demands of the captains—that is, the consumers—will replace him.

It is we as consumers who decide which companies shall prosper and which shall fail. We as consumers are bosses full of whims and fancies, changeable and unpredictable. When we see something we want and buy it, we do not care an iota about the past merit or vested interests of the person from whom we buy. If something is offered to us tomorrow better or cheaper, or both, we desert our old purveyor.

The old mousetrap story was true a hundred years ago and is true today. If we make the best one, and it is priced right, and we serve a thousand people—we prosper. If we serve a million and do it better than our mousetrap competitors, we prosper a thousand-fold. And not because we are capitalistic. We prosper only because we serve more people better than others, we satisfy their wants, we help them along the way.

The same harsh but fair criterion applies to those who sell their services. Those who work best, work hardest, do more than is expected of them rather than less, cannot help but profit more. All of us know that the most difficult task is getting enough people to do well what is expected of them, and eventually do it better than was expected. Those who keep it up are rewarded with greater opportunities— as well as responsibilities.

10 WAYS OF JOINING
'THE CORONARY CLUB'

Ten ways to get into "the coronary club" were given by
Dr. Kenneth Price, noted heart specialist, in a speech to
the National Association of Credit Management.

They are—

1—Go to the office Saturdays, evenings and holidays.

2—Take a briefcase home nights and review your troubles and worries.

3—Show up early next morning after a night meeting to
impress the boss.

4—Never eat restful, relaxing meals. Grab a "quickie" or
do business at lunch.

5—Look on fishing, hunting and golf as "a waste of time."

6—Keep in touch with the office during your vacations.

7—Don't delegate any authority.

8—When traveling, "work all day and drive all night," to
save time.

9—Accept all invitations to banquets and to join committees.

10—After your customers have gone to bed, sit up half
the night writing reports.

*A sound mind in a sound body is a short but full
description of a happy state in this world. He that
has these two, has little more to wish for; and he
that wants either of them, will be little the better
for anything else.* —JOHN LOCKE

*He had had much experience of physicians, and said,
"The only way to keep your health is to eat what you
don't want, drink what you don't like, and do what
you'd druther not."*
— MARK TWAIN, *Pudd'nhead Wilson*

*Hold fast then to this sound and wholesome rule of
life; indulge the body only so far as is needful for
health.* — SENECA

*If doctors fail you, let these three be your doctors:
A cheerful mind, rest, and moderate diet.*

The State of Ladies' Fashions
By MARK TWAIN

I ONCE MADE UP MY MIND to keep the ladies of the State of Nevada posted upon the fashions, but I found it hard to do. The fashions got so shaky that it was hard to tell what was good orthodox fashion, and what heretical and vulgar. This shakiness still obtains in everything pertaining to a lady's dress except her bonnet and her shoes. Some wear waterfalls, some wear nets, some wear cataracts of curls, and a few go bald, among the old maids; so no man can swear to any particular "fashion" in the matter of hair.

The same uncertainty seems to prevail regarding hoops. Little "high-flyer" schoolgirls of bad associations, and a good many women of full growth, wear no hoops at all. And we suspect these, as quickly and as naturally as we suspect a woman who keeps a poodle. Some who I know to be ladies, wear the ordinary moderate-sized hoop, and some who I also know to be ladies, wear the new hoop of the "spread-eagle" pattern—and some wear the latter who are not elegant and virtuous ladies—but that is a thing that may be said of any fashion whatever, of course.

The new hoops with a spreading base look only tolerably well. They are not bell-shaped—the "spread" is much more abrupt than that. It is tent-shaped; I do not mean any army tent, but a circus tent—which comes down steep and small half way and then shoots suddenly out horizontally and spreads abroad.

The beautiful is a phenomenon which is never apparent of itself, but is reflected in a thousand different works of the Creator.

— GOETHE

FROM SPOON RIVER ANTHOLOGY

by EDGAR LEE MASTERS

Do the boys and girls still go to Siever's
For cider, after school, in late September?
Or gather hazel nuts among the thickets
On Aaron Hatfield's farm when the frosts begin?
For many times with the laughing girls and boys
Played I along the road and over the hills
When the sun was low and the air was cool,
Stopping to club the walnut tree
Standing leafless against a flaming west.
Now, the smell of the autumn smoke,
And the dropping acorns,
And the echoes about the vales
Bring dreams of life. They hover over me.
They question me:
Where are those laughing comrades?
How many are with me, how many
In the old orchards along the way to Siever's,
And in the woods that overlook
The quiet water?

...as regards early rising

Early to bed, and early to rise,
Makes a man healthy, wealthy and wise.
—*Benjamin Franklin.*

I don't see it—George Washington.

Now BOTH OF THESE are high authorities—very high and respectable authorities—but I am with General Washington first, last, and all the time on this proposition.

Because I don't see it, either.

I have tried getting up early, and I have tried getting up late—and the latter agrees with me best. As for a man's growing any wiser, or any richer, or any healthier, by getting up early, I know it is not so; because I have got up early in the station-house many and many a time, and got poorer and poorer for the next half a day, in consequence, instead of richer and richer. And sometimes, on the same terms, I have seen the sun rise four times a week up there at Virginia, and so far from my growing healthier on account of it, I got to looking blue, and pulpy, and swelled, like a drowned man, and my relations grew alarmed and thought they were going to lose me. They entirely despaired of my recovery, at one time, and began to grieve for me as one whose day were numbered—whose fate was sealed—who was soon to pass away from them forever, and from the glad sunshine, and the birds, and the odorous flowers, and murmuring brooks, and whispering winds, and all the cheerful scenes of life, and go down into the dark and silent tomb—and they went forth sorrowing, and jumped a lot in the graveyard, and made up their minds to grin and bear it with that fortitude which is the true Christian's brightest ornament.

You observe that I have put a stronger test on the matter than even Benjamin Franklin contemplated, and yet it would not work. Therefore, how is a man to grow healthier, and wealthier, and wiser by going to bed early and getting up early, when he fails to accomplish these things even when he does not go to bed at all? And as far as becoming wiser is concerned, you might put all the wisdom I acquired in these experiments in your eye, without obstructing your vision any to speak of.

As I said before, my voice is with George Washington's on this question. —MARK TWAIN

SO IT GOES...
by
CARL SANDBURG
from Smoke and Steel

Every year Emily Dickinson sent one friend the first arbutus bud in her garden.

In a last will and testament Andrew Jackson remembered a friend with the gift of George Washington's pocket spyglass.

Napoleon too, in a last testament, mentioned a silver watch taken from the bedroom of Frederick the Great, and passed along this trophy to a particular friend.

O. Henry took a blood carnation from his coat lapel and handed it to a country girl starting work in a bean bazaar, and scribbled: "Peach blossoms may or may not stay pink in city dust."

So it goes. Some things we buy, some not. Tom Jefferson was proud of his radishes, and Abe Lincoln blacked his own boots, and Bismarck called Berlin a wilderness of brick and newspapers.

So it goes. There are accomplished facts.
Ride, ride, ride on in the great new blimps —
Cross unheard-of oceans, circle the planet.
When you come back we may sit by five hollyhocks.
We might listen to boys fighting for marbles.
The grasshopper will look good to us.

So it goes...

RULES IN
QUEEN ELIZABETH'S COURT

The Spiritual Glass

"Read distinctly.
Pray devoutly.
Sigh deeply.
Suffer patiently.
Make yourselves lowly.
Give not sentence hastily.
Speak but seldom, and that truly.
Prevent your speech discreetly.
Observe *Ten*[1] diligently.
Flee from *Seven*[2] mightily.
Guide *Five*[3] circumspectly.
Resist temptation strongly.
Break that off quickly.
Weep bitterly.
Have compassion tenderly.
Do good deeds lustily.
Love heartily.
Love faithfully.
Love God only.
Love all others for him charitably.
Love in adversity.
Love in prosperity.
Think always on Love, which is nothing
    but God himself.
Thus Love bringeth the Lover to Love,
    which is God himself."

[1]Commandments.
[2]Deadly Sins.
[3]Senses.

There are many moments of Friendship as in love, when silence is beyond words

There are many moments in friendship, as in love, when silence is beyond words. The faults of our friend may be clear to us, but it is well to seem to shut our eyes to them. Friendship is usually treated by the majority of mankind as a tough and everlasting thing which will survive all manner of bad treatment. But this is an exceedingly great and foolish error; it may die in an hour of a single unwise word; its conditions of existence are that it should be dealt with delicately and tenderly, being as it is a sensitive plant and not a roadside thistle. We must not expect our friend to be above humanity. — OUIDA

The man who will share his purse with you in the days of poverty and distress, and like the good Samaritan, be surety for your support to the landlord, you may admit to your confidence, incorporate into the very core of your heart, and call him friend; misfortunes cannot shake him from you; a prison will not conceal you from his sight. —J. BARTLETT

The love of man to woman is a thing common and of course, and at first partakes more of instinct and passion than choice; but true friendship between man and man is infinite and immortal. — PLATO

Think of the importance of friendship in the education of men. It will make a man honest; it will make him a hero; it will make him a saint. It is the state of the just dealing with the just, the magnanimous with the magnanimous, the sincere with the sincere, man with man.

—THOREAU

If a man does not make new acquaintances as he passes through life, he will soon find himself left alone. A man should keep his friendships in constant repair. —JOHNSON

Friendship that flows from the heart cannot be frozen by adversity, as the water that flows from the spring cannot congeal in winter.

—J. FENIMORE COOPER

We inherit our relatives and our features and may not escape them; but we can select our clothing and our friends, and let us be careful that both fit us. —VOLNEY STREAMER

A slender acquaintance with the world must convince every man that actions, not words, are the true criterion of the attachment of friends; and that the most liberal professions of goodwill are very far from being the surest marks of it. — GEORGE WASHINGTON

It is chance that makes brothers, but hearts that make friends.

A man's reputation is what his friends say about him. His character is what his enemies say about him.

SLEEPYHEADS

by
CARL SANDBURG
from Smoke and Steel

Sleep is a maker of makers. Birds sleep. Feet cling to a perch. Look at the balance. Let the legs loosen, the back-bone untwist, the head go heavy over, the whole works tumbles a done bird off the perch.

Fox cubs sleep. The pointed head curls round into hind legs and tail. It is a ball of red hair. It is a muff waiting. A wind might whisk it in the air across pastures and rivers, a cocoon, a pod of seeds. The snooze of the black nose is in a circle of red hair.

Old men sleep. In chimney corners, in rocking chairs, at wood stoves, steam radiators. They talk and forget and nod and are out of talk with closed eyes. Forgetting to live. Knowing the time has come useless for them to live. Old eagles and old dogs run and fly in the dreams.

Babies sleep. In flannels the papoose faces, the bambino noses, and dodo, dodo the song of many matushkas. Babies —a leaf on a tree in the spring sun. A nub of a new thing sucks the sap of a tree in the sun, yes a new thing, a what-is-it? A left hand stirs, an eyelid twitches, the milk in the belly bubbles and gets to be blood and a left hand and an eyelid. Sleep is a maker of makers.

Blessings on him that first invented sleep!
It covers a man, thoughts and all like a cloak;
It is meat for the hungry, drink for the thirsty,
heat for the cold, and cold for the hot. It is
the current coin that purchases cheaply all the
pleasures of the world, and the balance that
sets even king and shepherd, fool and sage.

— CERVANTES, *Don Quixote.*

CONFUCIUS' WISDOM

He said of a woman whose father-in-law, husband, and son had been killed by tigers, but who preferred to remain where she was, because the government was not oppressive, "Oppressive government is more cruel than a tiger."

He told one of his disciples to take a horse from his carriage, and present it in payment of the funeral expense of a friend, with whose family he had been condoling while on a journey. "I dislike," he said, "the thought of my tears not being followed by any thing."

In the majority of cases, conscience is an elastic and very flexible article, which will bear a deal of stretching, and adapt itself to a great variety of circumstances. Some people, by prudent management, and leaving it off piece by piece, like a flannel waistcoat in warm weather, even contrive in time, to dispense with it altogether; but there are others who can assume the garment and throw it off at pleasure; and this, being the greatest and most convenient improvement, is the one most in vogue.

— CHARLES DICKENS — *Old Curiosity Shop*

The world is my country, all mankind are my brethren, and to do good is my religion.

—THOMAS PAINE

Painting is the intermediate somewhat between a thought and a thing.

— SAMUEL TAYLOR COLERIDGE

You must look into people, as well as at them.

—LORD CHESTERFIELD

CHANT-ROYAL OF ROMANCE
THAT IS NOT DEAD:

ROMANCE is dead, say some, and so to-day
  Honor and Chivalry are faint and cold;
And now Adventure has no modern way
  To stir our blood, as in the days of old.
They mourn the day of Chivalry as done,
Knighthood has seen the setting of its sun,
That fairy, nymph and genie, grown too shy,
No more in these new days hold revels high;
  There lives no Mystery now, and they cry woe
To this old world, so twisted and awry.
  Romance is dead, say some,— but I say no!

Not while Youth lives, and Springtime bids be gay;
  Not while Love blooms, and lovers dare be bold;
Not while a poet sings his roundelay,
  And men by maidens' kisses are cajoled.
You have not seen her—or you, too, would shun
The thought that in this world Romance there's none,
For O, my Love, has power to beautify
My whole life long, and all its charm supply,—
  My love, my youth, my dreams, to her I owe!
And so, ye scornful cynics, I deny;—
  Romance is dead, say some,— but I say no!

ENVOY

God, keep my youth and love alive, that I
May wonder at this world until I die;
  Let sea and mountain speak to me, that so
Waking or sleeping, I may fight the lie;—
  Romance is dead, say some,— but I say no!

STEER THE BOAT!

Story of the Voyageurs

Of the Canadian voyageurs or engagees, a race that has now so nearly passed away, some notice may very properly here be given.

They were unlike any other class of men. Like the poet, they seemed born to their vocation. Sturdy, enduring, ingenious, and light-hearted, they possessed a spirit capable of adapting itself to any emergency. No difficulties baffled, no hardships discouraged them; while their affectionate nature led them to form attachments of the warmest character to their "bourgeois," or master, as well as to the native inhabitants, among whom their engagements carried them.

Montreal, or, according to their own pronunciation, *Marrialle,* was their depot. It was at that place that the agents commissioned to make up the quota for the different companies and traders found the material for their selections.

The terms of engagement were usually from four to six hundred livres (ancient Quebec currency) per annum as wages, with rations of one quart of lyed corn, and two ounces of tallow per diem, or "its equivalent in whatever sort of food is to be found in the Indian country." Instances have been known of their submitting cheerfully to fare upon fresh fish and maple-sugar for a whole winter, when cut off from other supplies.

It was a common saying, "Keep an engagee to his corn and tallow, he will serve you well—give him pork and bread, and he soon gets beyond your management." They regard the terms of their engagement as binding to the letter. An old trader, M. Berthelet, engaged a crew at Montreal. The terms of agreement were, that they should eat when their bourgeois did, and what he did. It was a piece of fun on the part of the old gentleman, but the simple Canadians believed it to be a signal instance of good luck that had provided them such luxurious prospects. The bourgeois stuffed his pockets with crackers, and, when sure of being quite unobserved, would slily eat one. Pipe after pipe passed—the men grew hungry, but, observing that there were no preparations of a meal for the bourgeois, they bore their fast without complaining.

At length the matter became too serious—they could stand it no longer. In their distress they begged off from the bargain, and gladly compounded to take the customary rations, instead of the dainty fare they had been promising themselves with their master.

On arriving at Mackinac, which was the entrepot of the fur trade, a small proportion of the voyageur's wages was advanced him, to furnish his winter's outfit, his pipes and tobacco, his needles and thread, some pieces of bright-colored ribbons, and red and yellow gartering (quality binding), with which to purchase their little necessaries from the Indians. To these, if his destination were Lake Superior, or a post far to the north where such articles could not be readily obtained, were added one or two smoked deer-skins for moccasins.

Thus equipped, he entered upon his three years' service, to toil by day, and laugh, joke, sing, and tell stories when the evening hour brought rest and liberty.

There was not wanting here and there an instance of obstinate adherence to the exact letter of the agreement in regard to the nature of employment, although, as a general thing, the engagee held himself ready to fulfil the behests of his bourgeois, as faithfully as ever did vassal those of his chief.

A story is told of M. St. Jean, a trader on the Upper Mississippi, who upon a certain occasion ordered one of his Frenchmen to accompany a party to the forest to chop wood. The man refused. "He was not hired," he said, "to chop wood."

"Ah! for what, then, were you hired?"

"To steer a boat."

"Very well; steer a boat, then, since you prefer it."

It was mid-winter. The recusant was marched to the riverside, and placed in the stern of the boat, which lay fastened in the ice.

After serving a couple of hours at his legitimate employment, with the thermometer below zero, he was quite content to take his place with the chopping-party, and never again thought it good policy to choose work for himself.

A DAUGHTER'S LOVE FOR HER FATHER

"I had rather not live, than not to
be the daughter of such a man!"

An impartial study of Burr and Hamilton will convince
any unprejudiced mind that Burr was at least Hamilton's
equal, if not his superior, as a soldier, orator, scholar, lawyer,
and politician. They were about the same age; they held
the same rank in the army; they were both members of
Washington's military household; apparently their chances
in the race of life were equal, if there were any difference
Burr's were rather the better; but, for reasons satisfactory
to himself, Washington gave to Hamilton, the West Indian
adventurer, his love and confidence, both of which he resolutely withheld from Burr, the child of New England Puri-
tans; and, in so doing, such was his vast influence over his
contemporaries, started one on the broad highway to success, and the other upon the broader and easier road to
infamy.

If Burr was without integrity as Washington thought,
if he had a bad heart and no conscience as the world now
believes, what becomes of the well-developed and carefully
cherished theory of heredity? How can philosophers and
psychologists explain the astounding fact that the son of
President Burr, of Princeton, whose virtues were the re-
sounding theme of every tongue,– the grandson of Jonathan
Edwards, the well-nigh perfect man,– how can they explain
the indubitable fact that their descendant, the heir of numerous generations of Puritan conscience and New England
excellence, should be the sinner paramount of his age? This
problem is worthy of their profoundest consideration. That
in the beginning of his career and the morning of his fame
his kinship to these people helped him, no sane man can
doubt,– old John Adams says it was his chief stock in trade,
and that the same fact stands as a heavy item against him
in his final account with mankind is equally clear. They
make it in him a matter of guilt that in his veins flowed the
blood of the Psalm-singing Roundheads who charged with
Oliver at Naseby, Marston Moor, and Dunbar, shouting,
"God with us!"

In this brilliant man's entire character there is but one redeeming feature – he loved his only child, the beautiful and gifted Theodosia, with a fervor and devotion rarely equaled and never excelled. Whatever of heart he possessed, he lavished upon her; his care, his solicitude, his labor for her was enthusiastic and unceasing; and she repaid him in Scripture measure – "heaped up, pressed down, and running over." In the midst of his misfortunes, in the deepest of his ignominy, when the vast majority of his countrymen were clamoring for his blood, she writes him daily and hourly bidding him be of good cheer, while she is hastening to his beloved presence, to stand by his side in the prisoner's dock and share his quarters in the Richmond penitentiary.

In one of her tender epistles to him she says: "I had rather not live than not to be the daughter of such a man," as Aaron Burr! All history presents no attachment stronger than that of this fallen archangel and Theodosia. David and Jonathan, Damon and Pythias – these have been celebrated themes for orators and poets from a time whereof the memory of man runneth not to the contrary. But they were strong men, – veteran soldiers. Theodosia Alston's love for her father overtops them all and half-redeems his fame; for it stands to reason and to nature that there must have been something good in a man who could inspire such deathless affection in a heart so pure as hers. She died at last in an effort and on a voyage to once more clasp him to her faithful breast, when, loaded with infamy, he was shunned and cursed by all mankind and had become a hissing and a by-word in the mouth of the civilized world. Her death, awful in its mystery, impossible to think of even now without a shudder, was the only thing that ever melted his hard heart or humbled his defiant soul amid countless calamities and through forty years of the most terrible punishment ever inflicted on any of the sons of Adam.

An undutiful daughter will prove an unmanageable wife.

—BENJAMIN FRANKLIN, *Poor Richard*

"I have had my season of frolic in youth"

I have loved and run riot like all the world—
    Who knows not riot and love?
Through my heart the storms of passions have whirled,
    The frenzy from heaven above.

Now away with it all! For the hoar-white hair
    Is thrusting the sable away,
And a message is come and a sign to declare
    'Tis time to be sober today.

I have had my season of frolic in youth,
    And now that the season is past,
'Tis time to bethink me of wisdom forsooth,
    'Tis time for reforming at last.   —PHILODEMUS

It is never too late to tread the path to honesty.
          —SENECA

*Except such men think themselves wiser
than Cicero for teaching of eloquence, they
must be content to turn a new leaf.*
    —ROGER ACHAM, *Scholemaster* (1570)

*He bought a Bible of the new translation,
And in his life he show'd great reformation;
He walked mannerly and talked meekly;
He heard three lectures and two sermons weekly;
He vow'd to shun all companies unruly,
And in his speech he used no oath but "truly."*
    —SIR JOHN HARRINGTON, *Of A Precise Tailor*

WILLIAM CLARK   MERIWETHER LEWIS

Reproduced from the Engraving, after St. Memin's Miniature

THE TRAIL OF LEWIS AND CLARK

Colter was also the principal figure in one of the most remarkable adventures that ever befell any man. It is one of those cases where truth surpasses fiction and the episode deserves recounting here in full. It is a picture of a time now gone and that can never be duplicated in this country. The tale was originally told by Bradbury, to whom Colter himself related it, and is given in his *Travels in the Interior of America*, 2d edition, London, 1819, a volume rare in more senses than one:

This man came to St. Louis in May, 1810, in a small canoe, from the head waters of the Missouri, a distance of three thousand miles, which he traversed in thirty days. I saw him on his arrival, and received from him an account of his adventures after he had separated from Lewis and Clarke's party: one of these, from its singularity, I shall relate. On the arrival of the party on the head waters of the Missouri, Colter, observing an appearance of abundance of beaver being there, he got permission to remain and hunt for some time, which he did in company with a man of the name of Dixon, who had traversed the immense tract of country from St. Louis to the head waters of the Missouri alone. Soon after he separated from Dixon, and *trapped* in company with a hunter named Potts; and aware of the hostility of the Blackfeet Indians, one of whom had been killed by Lewis, they set their traps at night, and took them up early in the morning, remaining concealed during the day. They were examining their traps early one morning, in a creek about six miles from that branch of the Missouri called Jefferson's Fork, and were ascending in a canoe, when they suddenly heard a great noise, resembling the trampling of animals; but they could not ascertain the fact, as the high perpendicular banks on each side of the river impeded their view. Colter immediately pronounced it to be occasioned by Indians, and advised an instant retreat; but was accused of cowardice by Potts, who insisted that the noise was caused by buffaloes, and they proceeded on.

Retreat was now impossible

In a few minutes afterwards their doubts were removed, by a party of Indians making their appearance on both sides of the creek, to the amount of five or six hundred, who beckoned them to come ashore. As retreat was now impossible, Colter turned the head of the canoe to the shore; and at the moment of its touching, an Indian seized the rifle belonging to Potts; but Colter, who is a remarkably strong man, immediately retook it, and handed it to Potts, who remained in the canoe, and on receiving it pushed off into the river. He had scarcely quitted the shore when an arrow was shot at him, and he cried out, *"Colter, I am wounded."* Colter remonstrated with him on the folly of attempting to escape, and urged him to come ashore. Instead of complying, he instantly levelled his rifle at an Indian, and shot him dead on the spot. This conduct, situated as he was, may appear to have been an act of madness; but it was doubtless the effect of sudden, but sound reasoning; for if

INDIAN UTENSILS AND ARMS

taken alive, he must have expected to be tortured to death, according to their custom. He was instantly pierced with arrows so numerous, that, to use the language of Colter, "*he was made a riddle of.*"

They now seized Colter, stripped him entirely naked, and began to consult on the manner in which he should be put to death. They were first inclined to set him up as a mark to shoot at; but the chief interfered, and seizing him by the shoulder, asked him if he could run fast. Colter, who had been some time amongst the Kee-kat-sa, or Crow Indians, had in a considerable degree acquired the Blackfoot language, and was also well acquainted with Indian customs. He knew that he had now to run for his life, with the dreadful odds of five or six hundred against him, and those armed Indians; therefore cunningly replied that he was a very bad runner, although he was considered by the hunters as remarkably swift. The chief now commanded the party to remain stationary, and led Colter out on the prairie three or four hundred yards, and released him, bidding him *to save himself if he could.* At that instant the horrid war whoop sounded in the ears of poor Colter, who, urged with the hope of preserving life, ran with a speed at which he was himself surprised. He proceeded towards the Jefferson Fork, having to traverse a plain six miles in breadth, abounding with the prickly pear, on which he was every instant treading with his naked feet. He ran nearly half way across the plain before he ventured to look over his shoulder, when he perceived that the Indians were very much scattered, and that he had gained ground to a considerable distance from the main body; but one Indian, who carried a spear, was much before all the rest, and not more than a hundred yards from him. A faint gleam of hope now cheered the heart of Colter: he derived confidence from the belief that escape was within the bounds of possibility; but that confidence was nearly being fatal to him, for he exerted himself to such a degree, that the blood gushed from his nostrils, and soon almost covered the fore part of his body.

He distinctly heard the appalling sound of footsteps

He had now arrived within a mile of the river, when he distinctly heard the appalling sound of footsteps behind him, and every instant expected to feel the spear of his pursuer. Again he turned his head, and saw the savage not twenty yards from him. Determined if possible to avoid the expected blow, he suddenly stopped, turned round, and spread out his arms. The Indian, surprised by the suddenness of the action, and perhaps at the bloody appearance of Colter, also attempted to stop; but exhausted with running, he fell whilst endeavoring to throw his spear, which stuck in the ground, and broke in his hand. Colter instantly snatched up the pointed part, with which he pinned him to the earth, and then continued his flight. The foremost of the Indians, on arriving at the place, stopped till others came up to join them, when they set up a hideous yell. Every moment of this time was improved by Colter, who, although fainting and exhausted, succeeded in gaining the skirting of the cotton wood trees, on the borders of the fork, through which he ran, and plunged into the river. Fortunately for him, a little below this place there was an island, against the upper point of which a raft of drift timber had lodged. He dived under the raft, and after several efforts, got his head above water amongst the trunks of trees, covered over with smaller wood to the depth of several feet. Scarcely had he secured himself, when the Indians arrived on the river, screeching and yelling, as Colter expressed it, "like so many devils." They were frequently on the raft during the day, and were seen through the chinks by Colter, who was congratulating himself on his escape, until the idea arose that they might set the raft on fire.

His situation was still dreadful

In horrible suspense he remained until night, when hearing no more of the Indians, he dived from under the raft, and swam silently down the river to a considerable distance, when he landed and travelled all night. Although happy in having escaped from the Indians, his situation was still dreadful: he was completely naked, under a burning sun; the soles of his feet were entirely filled with the thorns of the prickly pear; he was hungry, and had no means of killing game, although he saw abundance around him, and was at least seven days journey from Lisa's Fort, on the Bighorn branch of the Roche Jaune River. These were circumstances under which almost any man but an American hunter would have despaired. He arrived at the fort in seven days, having subsisted on a root much esteemed by the Indians of the Missouri, now known by naturalists as *psoralea esculenta*.

It may easily be imagined that such an experience might cool one's desire for life in a wild region and break one's constitution.

SUFFICIENCY

I care not for the lands with pastures deep,
  Nor wealth of gold with jealous eyes I see;
Nor, having what's enough, I more would reap.
  Too much of anything's too much for me!

—ALPHEUS OF MITYLENE

HOARDED WEALTH

Thou gatherest wealth—what profit shall it be?
Canst drag thy riches to the grave with thee?
Thou barterest time for gold—hast thou the power
To heap up life, or buy one added hour?

—PALLADAS

YOUTH AND RICHES

Young, I was poor; when old, I wealthy grew;
  Unblest, alas! in want and plenty too!
When I could all enjoy, fate nothing gave;
  Now I can nought enjoy, I all things have.

GOLD

Some take their gold
In minted mold,
And some in harps hereafter,
But give me mine
In tresses fine,
And keep the change in laughter!

— OLIVER HERFORD

There is nothing truly valuable which can
be purchased without pains and labor.

—THE TATLER

THE WEATHER DEPARTMENT

"Well, Duncombe, how will be the weather?"
"Sir, it looks cloudy altogether,
And coming across our Houghton Green,
I stopped and talked with old Frank Beane.
While we stood there, sir, old Jan Swain
Went by and said he knowed 'twould rain;
The next that came was Master Hunt,
And he declared he knew it wouldn't.
And then I met with Farmer Blow,
He plainly said he didn't know,
So, sir, when doctors disagree,
Who's to decide it, you or me?"

Too hot to sleep, too hot to lie,
Too hot to laugh, too hot to cry,
Too hot to stand, too hot to sit,
Too hot to sew, too hot to knit,
Too hot to ride, too hot to walk,
Too hot to read, too hot to talk,
Too hot to eat, too hot to drink,
Too hot to write, too hot to think,
Too hot to scold, too hot to tease,
Too hot to cough, too hot to sneeze,
Too hot to play, too hot to sing,
Too hot, too hot, for anything.

And when a man of fifty finds his corns
Ache and his joints throb, and foresees a storm,
Though neighbors laugh and say the sky is clear,
Let us henceforth believe him weatherwise.
— ROBERT BROWNING

What is more gentle than a wind in summer?
—JOHN KEATS

THE SEASONS

(from lusty Spring to Winter, cloathed all in frize)

So forth issued the seasons of the year;
First, lusty Spring, all dight in leaves of flowers
That freshly budded, and new blooms did bear,
In which a thousand birds had built their bowers.

Then came jolly Summer, being dight
In a thin silken cassock, colored green,
That was unlined, all to be more light,
And on his head a garland well beseene.

Then came the Autumn all in yellow clad,
As though he joyed in his plenteous store,
Laden with fruits that made him laugh, full glad
That he had banished hunger, which to-fore
Had by the belly oft him pinched sore:
Upon his head a wreath, that was enroll'd
With ears of corn of every sort, he bore;
And in his hand a sickle he did hold,
To reap the ripen'd fruits the which the earth
  had yold.

Lastly came Winter cloathed all in frize,
Chattering his teeth for cold that did him chill;
Whilst on his hoary beard his breath did freeze,
And the dull drops that from his purple bill
As from a limbeck did adown distill;
In his right hand a tipped staff he held
With which his feeble steps he stayed still,
For he was faint with cold and weak with eld,
That scarce his loosed limbs he able was to weld.

— EDMUND SPENSER — *The Faerie Queene*

another version

Spring: slippy, drippy, nippy,
Summer: showery, flowery, bowery.
Autumn: hoppy, croppy, poppy.
Winter: wheezy, sneezy, breezy.

INDIAN WAR DESPATCH

The following is a *facsimile* of a gazette of a tribe of North American Indians, who assisted the French forces in Canada, during the war between France and England:—

Explanation of the Gazette, giving an account of one of their expeditions. The following divisions explain those on the plate, as referred to by the numbers:—

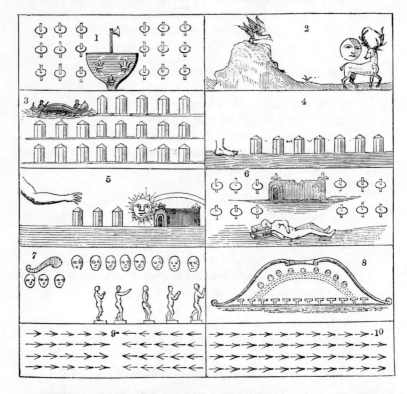

1. Each of these figures represents the number ten. They all signify, that 18 times 10, or 180 American Indians, took up the hatchet, or declared war, in favor of the French, which is represented by the hatchet placed over the arms of France.

2. They departed from Montreal—represented by the bird just taking wing from the top of a mountain. The moon and the buck show the time to have been in the first quarter of the buck-moon, answering to July.

3. They went by water—signified by the canoe. The number of huts, such as they raise to pass the night in, shows they were 21 days on their passage.

4. Then they came on shore, and traveled seven days by land—represented by the foot and the seven huts.

5. When they arrived near the habitations of their enemies, at sunrise—shown by the sun being to the eastward of them, beginning, as they think, its daily course, there they lay in wait three days—represented by the hand pointing, and the three huts.

6. After which, they surprised their enemies, in number 12 times 10, or 120. The man asleep shows how they surprised them, and the hole in the top of the building is supposed to signify that they broke into some of their habitations in that manner.

7. They killed with the club eleven of their enemies, and took five prisoners. The former represented by the club and the eleven heads, the latter by the figures on the little pedestals.

8. They lost nine of their own men in the action—represented by the nine heads within the bow, which is the emblem of honor among the Americans, but had none taken prisoners—a circumstance they lay great weight on, shown by all the pedestals being empty.

9. The heads of the arrows, pointing opposite ways, represent the battle.

10. The heads of the arrows all pointing the same way, signify the flight of the enemy.

"Jim."

SAY there! P'r'aps
Some on you chaps
　　Might know Jim Wild?
Well,– no offence:
Thar ain't no sense
　　In gittin' riled!

Jim was my chum
　　Up on the Bar:
That's why I come
　　Down from up yar,
Lookin' for Jim.
Thank ye, sir! *You*
Ain't of that crew,–
　　Blest if you are!

Money? – Not much:
　　That ain't my kind:
I ain't no such.
　　Rum? – I don't mind,
Seein' it's you.

Well, this yer Jim,
Did you know him? –

Jess 'bout your size;
Same kind of eyes;–
Well, that is strange:
　　Why, it's two year
　　Since he came here,
Sick, for a change.

Well, here's to us:
   Eh?
The h – – you say!
   Dead?
That little cuss?

What makes you star,–
You over thar?
Can't a man drop
's glass in yer shop
But you must rar'?
   It wouldn't take
   D – – much to break
You and your bar.

      Dead!
Poor – little – Jim!
Why, thar was me,
Jones, and Bob Lee,
Harry and Ben,–
No-account men:
Then to take *him!*

Well, thar – Good by,–
No more, sir,– I –
   Eh?
What's that you say? –

Why, dern it! – sho! –
No? Yes! By Joe!
   Sold!
Sold! Why, you limb,
You ornery,
      Derned old
Long-legged Jim!

BREVITY IS A VIRTUE

Abraham Lincoln's only autobiography was written in 1848 at the request of Charles Lanman, who was then making up his "Dictionary of Congress," and had asked Mr. Lincoln for a sketch of his life. The following is Abraham Lincoln's written reply: "Born February 12, 1809, in Hardin County, Kentucky. Education, defective. Profession, lawyer. Have been a captain of volunteers in the Black Hawk War. Postmaster at a very small office. Four times a member of the Illinois legislature. And was a member of the lower House of Congress. Yours, etc., A. Lincoln."

FIXING THE BLAME

After Lee had taken Harper's Ferry, the President, realizing how great a calamity it was to the Northern arms, determined, if possible, to fix the responsibility. Halleck was summoned, but did not know where the blame lay. "Very well," said Lincoln, "I'll ask General Schenck." The latter could throw no light upon the question further than to say he was not to blame. Milroy was the next to be called to the presence of the Commander-in-chief, and to enter a plea of "not guilty." Hooker was next given a hearing, and "Fighting Joe" made an emphatic disclaimer of all responsibility. Then the President assembled the four in his room, and said: "Gentlemen, Harper's Ferry was surrendered, and none of you, it seems, is responsible. I am very anxious to discover who is." After striding across the room several times, the President suddenly threw up his bowed head and exclaimed, "I have it! I know who is responsible." "Who, Mr. President; who is it?" anxiously inquired the distinguished quartet. "Gentlemen," said the President, "General Lee is the man."

TWELVE GOOD RULES

by KING CHARLES I

1. Urge no healths.
2. Profane no divine ordnances.
3. Touch no state matters.
4. Reveal no secrets.
5. Pick no quarrels.
6. Make no comparisons.
7. Maintain no ill opinions.
8. Keep no bad company.
9. Encourage no vice.
10. Make no long meals.
11. Repeat no grievances.
12. Lay no wagers.

"Build a little fence of trust"

Build a little fence of trust
   around today;
Fill the space with loving work,
   and therein stay;
Look not through the sheltering bars
   upon tomorrow;
God will help thee bear what comes
   of jor or sorrow.

       —MARY FRANCES BUTTS.

Men are not flattered by being shown
that there has been a difference of
purpose between the Almighty and them.

   ABRAHAM LINCOLN, *Letter to Thurlow Weed.*

Dr. Tom Dooley Writes a Letter to a Young Doctor

Written for Think Magazine and is reprinted by permission (Copyright, 1961, by International Business Machine corporation). Courtesy MED-ICO INC. Following is a condensation of Dr. Dooley's "letter to a young doctor.")

By DR. THOMAS A. DOOLEY

Village of Muong Sing
Kingdom of Laos

Dear:

It is far past midnight. I am sitting at the table in a House at Muong Sing high in the foothills of the Himalayas in northern Laos. The kerosene pressure lamps overhead are hissing at me, and the wind is lashing down my valley. It whips the palm and frangipani. All the earth on this sad cut of the world seems flooded in the monsoon rains. This is the season of the crashing violence of the tropical storm. The crickets, frogs, and wilder jungle animals scream and scream. The high Laos night land is not calm.

But I feel very calm in writing to you. I feel as tho I have just met you outside of the medical school auditorium. May I thrust my hand out and say, "Congratulations, Bart. Congratulations on your graduation from medical school. Congratulations on being a doctor."

Time of Indecision

Bart, you've a year's internship ahead of you. And after that, the choice of a residency for specialty training or private practice. I know you have been plagued with some indecision, "Shall I be a specialist with years and years of more training or shall I go into private practice now?"

I am going to presume that you will choose the life of a general practitioner. There is a place in the world for specialists [speaketh the young G. P.], but this battered, beaten world of ours needs a few more country doctors in even a few more countries and villages too.

As a general practitioner, where will you practice? There is a need for you every place. But the world is all lopsided in its distribution of doctors. Almost all corners of America have available doctors.

Available to All

With veteran's benefits, social security, labor union programs, industrial group health plans, and all the others, there is hardly a citizen who cannot find medical attention if he is willing to make some little effort.

I live in Laos. This valley, prior to our Medico hospital, had nothing but black magic, necromancy, witchcraft, clay images, sorcery, and betel juice. The villagers wallowed in monkey's blood, cob-webs, tigers' teeth, and incantations. They never had hope, much less help. Today, the people of Muong Sing have good medicine, compassionate help, training, and a fine little 25 bed hospital.

Statistics Are Staggering

You know the world's statistics. The Congo, 13 million people and not one native doctor. South Viet Nam, 11 million people, about 180 doctors. Cambodia, 5 million people, seven doctors. Laos, 3 million people, one Lao doctor. Other nations' statistics are equally staggering. . . .

Bart, I believe that the unique aspect of this challenge to young doctors demands that we invest some of our lives in the practice of medicine in foreign fields. I say "some," not a lifetime. This is not expected of us. But we can give a year or two. It can be part of the maturation of a man, the metamorphosis of a doctor.

You went thru college, medical school, clerkship, internship lies ahead, maybe residency, and then . . . come to the developing nations of the world for a while. Bring your gadgets, and the armamentarium of drugs, to be sure, but most of all bring your human spirit.

Bring alone a sense of humor, don't forget it; you'll certainly need it when the roof leaks, the patients eat all the pills the first dosage, and the witch doctors put cow dung over your sterile compresses. Bring also a few cents' worth of the spirit of adventure that our founding fathers possessed. . . .

Give Life to Others

Dedicate some of your life to others. Your dedication will not be a sacrifice. It will be an exhilerating experience because it is intense effort applied toward a meaningful end.

So along with my congratulations on your graduation I send my wish that you will utilize yourself as a force of unity in the fragile peace of today. And that you will know the happiness that comes of serving others who have nothing.

Sincere best wishes always,

TOM

As true olf Chaucer sang to us, so many years ago,
He is the gentlest man who dares the gentlest deeds to do:
However rude his birth or state, however low his place,
He is the gentle man whose life right gentle thought doth
    grace.
He is one of Nature's Gentlemen, the best of every time.

What though his hand is hard and rough with years of honest
    pains,—
Who ever thought the knight disgraced by honor's weather-
    stains?
What though no Herald's College in their books his line can
    trace,—
We can see that he is gentle by the smile upon his face.
For he's one of Nature's Gentlemen, the best of every time.

—W. J. LINTON
"Nature's Gentleman"

RIDE HIM!

By JOHN C. FROHLICHER

He may act all sweet and gentle but he's dynamite
    inside,
So don't you go to nodding when you take that
    prairie ride!
He'll jump sideways at a shadow if he finds your
    rein is loose,
You don't want to go a-trusting no spooky old
    cayuse!

There he goes! One lone jackrabbit sets him straight
    up in the air,
Crack your quirt across the withers! Use your spurs
    and lift some hair!
Work his head up to the saddle, get him stretched
    out in a run,
(One skitter-tailed jackrabbit is what started all
    the fun!)

Better ride him to a frazzle till his tail is flat and
    draggin'
(Tain't so pleasant to be grounded seven miles from
    the wagon!)
But there's mighty little difference twixt range
    hosses and range men –
When you think you've got them gentled you will
    find they're cocked again!

LUMBERJACK'S DEATH

By JOHN C. FROHLICHER

Where that one pine tree's rough-barked bole
Stands singing low beside that bouldered brook
There will you carry me.
You need not dig so very deep a hole,
And use not either candle, bell or book
There when you bury me;
But once more let your wild, mad voices roll
In river-driver's song; then, in that nook
Silence shall marry me.

PHUN WITH A PHONE BOOK
Reprint by permission of J. W. Clement Co.

There is plenty of *Beer* in your phone book. Also plenty of *Rye* and *Scotch*. If you're on the wagon you can have all the *Milks* you want. And your phone book probably has a *Center*, a *Bottom* and a *Topp*.

We are referring, of course, to the surnames of people. And we are assuming that your phone book is that of a big city.

If it is, you will be amazed at the variety of surnames you can find. And if you are a cross word puzzle fan, an anagram addict or just like to play with words, you can have fun and games with your phone book.

We worked out these samples in a couple of hours one afternoon when the boss wasn't looking. So help us, all the italicized words are personal surnames from our phone book. We considered the use of commercial or coined names not cricket.

We began by collecting the names of things. We found countries: *America, Canada, England, France, Holland, Denmark* and *Armenia*. Under fruits there were: *Berry, Lemon, Orange, Apple, Cherry* and *Plumb*. Naturally there were the common colors: *Black, Green, White, Brown* and *Gray*. But we also discovered people named *Scarlett, Tan, Blue, Buff* and *Pink*. We found a man named *Bird* and added: *Peacock, Wren, Robin, Thrush, Quail, Bunting, Thrasher, Cardinal, Lark* and *Finch*. Under royalty our book listed: *King, Kaiser, Lord, Prince, Princess, Queen, Count* and *Duke*.

Next we tried combining surnames and came up with: *Crimes Judge; General Officer; Hall Porter; Main Chance; Canny Scott; Slaven Master; Sweet Candy; Castle Moats; Salmon Fisher; Glass Ware;* and (ugh) *Limberg Cheesman.*

By placing an ampersand between names we invented. *Hill & Dale; Nutt & Bolt; Warr & Peace; Quarles & Fites;*

Coward & Braverman; and (for mosquito time) *Swatt & Sweat.* We sadly discarded *Hell & Heavern.*

Having gone this far we attempted to make sentences from surnames. These examples show it can be done, stretching a point here and there: *Winters Colden Summers Hotte. Brooks Fall Down Hill. Parker House Rolls Goes Good. Weir Wheeling Round Canaan.*

This educational essay proves two things. First, any big phone book is full of weird and wonderful surnames. Second, you will always have something to do if you have a phone book.

THE GARDEN OF
YOUR BUSINESS

THE NATIONAL INDEPENDENT LABOR JOURNAL—*June—1960*

First, plant four rows of peas:
Presence, promptness, preparation and perseverance.
Next to these plant three rows of squash:
Squash gossip, squash indifference, squash criticism.
Then plant five rows of lettuce:
Let us obey rules and regulations.
Let us be true to our obligations.
Let us be faithful to duty.
Let us be loyal and unselfish.
Let us love one another.
No garden is complete without turnips:
Turn up for meetings.
Turn up with a smile.
Turn up with new ideas.
Turn up with determination to make everything count for something good and worthwhile.

PEARL HARBOR

by John C. Frohlicher

They'll never fish again in quiet inland lakes,
Nor run, ski-shod, down slopes all powder snow;
They'll not dash up to lights with squealing brakes
Nor will they plow the plains where wheat crops grow.
They cannot touch, with well-remembered hands,
Or watch their children laughing home from school;
They'll read no news, hear no more booming bands,
Write no more glorious books, forge no more tool.
They'll never see their bright ambitions crumble
When sure and slow the tides of time have rolled—
They'll never have to learn how to be humble.
They lived in pride. They never will grow old.

Time brings not death, it brings but changes;
I know he rides but rides afar,
Today some other planet ranges
And camps tonight upon a star
Where all his other comrades are.

—Douglas Malloch, *A Comrade Rides Ahead.*

My sword I give to him that shall succeed me in my
pilgrimage, and my courage and skill to him that can
get it. My marks and scars I carry with me, to be a
witness for me that I have fought his battles who now
will be my rewarder. When the day that he must go hence
was come, many accompanied him to the riverside, into
which as he went he said: "Death, where is thy sting?"
And as he went down deeper he said: "Grave where is thy
victory?" So he passed over, and all the trumpets
sounded for him on the other side.

—Bunyan, *The Pilgrims Progress.*

"Thus scorning all the cares That fate or fortune brings"...

THE UPRIGHT LIFE

The man of life upright,
    Whose guiltless heart is free
From all dishonest deeds,
    Or thought of vanity;

The man whose silent days
    In harmless joys are spent,
Whom hopes cannot delude
    Nor sorrow discontent:

That man needs neither towers
    Nor armour for defence,
Nor secret vaults to fly
    From thunder's violence:

He only can behold
    With unaffrighted eyes
The horrors of the deep
    And terrors of the skies.

Thus scorning all the cares
    That fate or fortune brings,
He makes the heaven his book,
    His wisdom heavenly things;

Good thoughts his only friends,
    His wealth a well-spent age,
The earth his sober inn
    And quiet pilgrimage.

—Thomas Campion

TALENTS DIFFER
(A FABLE)

The mountain and the squirrel
Had a quarrel,
And the former called the latter "Little Prig";
Bun replied,
"You are doubtless very big;
But all sorts of things and weather
Must be taken in together,
To make up a year
And a sphere.
And I think it no disgrace
To occupy my place.
If I'm not so large as you,
You are not so small as I,
And not half so spry.
I'll not deny you make
A very pretty squirrel track;
Talents differ; all is well and wisely put;
If I cannot carry forests on my back,
Neither can you crack a nut."

RALPH WALDO EMERSON

Hide not your talents, they for use were made.
What's a Sun-dial in the Shade?
—BENJAMIN FRANKLIN, *Poor Richard*

TO RICH GIVERS

First published in 1860 by WALT WHITMAN

What you give me, I cheerfully accept,
A little sustenance, a hut and garden, a little money –
    these, as I rendezvous with my poems;
A traveler's lodging and breakfast as I journey through
    The States – Why should I be ashamed to own such
    gifts? Why to advertise for them?
For I myself am not one who bestows nothing upon man
    and woman;
For I bestow upon any man or woman the entrance to all
    the gifts of the universe.

PLEASURES ARE LIKE
SNOW FALLING IN THE RIVER

But pleasures are like poppies spread,
You seize the flow'r, it's bloom is shed!
Or like the snow falls in the river,
A moment white—then melts forever;
Or like the borealis race,
That flit ere you can point their place;
Or like the rainbow's lovely form,
Evanishing amid the storm.

"I am content with what I have,
Little be it, or much."
                    —BUNYAN

"THE WINNAHS — AND STILL CHAMPIONS!"

by John C. Frohlicher

It was a fight that couldn't happen today. The heavyweight championship of the world—being decided at Shelby, on the high Montana prairies! Jack Dempsey had agreed to fight Tom Gibbons there for a quarter of a million dollars, and 50% of the gate receipts, that July 4, 1923.

Dempsey got $200,000—and half the banks in Northern Montana were bent. About 8,000 people saw the fight, including the townspeople who tore down the fences and crowded right up to ringside. And Tommy Gibbons, the pride of St. Paul, Minnesota, never got a dime.

The fight was an exhibition of skill that men remember all their lives. For 15 rounds Gibbons stayed away from the "killer," the "Manassa Mauler," the most ruthless and efficient fighting machine the ring had ever known. "Hitting Tom" said Dempsey many years later "was like trying to thread a needle in a cyclone."

But while Dempsey kept the title, two champions—two world champions—walked out of that ring and went their ways, into the waiting years and to increasing glory.

Look at Jack Dempsey. Villified for no good reason as a slacker in World War I, he joined the Coast Guard in 1942, at the age of 47. Hundreds of young men learned how to protect themselves in the clinches—not the polite clinches of the prize ring but the deadly clinches of armed conflict. Dempsey finished the war with ribbons from the European, Asiatic, Pacific and African Theatres—and with the Legion of Merit. More, he was urged to finish out his life in the Coast Guard, making that his career.

In the long time since Shelby, Dempsey remained the "Champ." He earned this title after he lost the belt; no matter who holds the actual title, Jack will be known as the "Champ." His business ventures have earned him other respect too. And his actions, through the years, have gained him the affection of millions. He lost his crown to Gene Tunney—but he still is the idol of American fans.

Tommy Gibbons went on to glory, too. To glory in his own home town, in his home state of Minnesota. He had a notable ring career behind him when he hung up his gloves in 1925. The preceding twelve years, as a middleweight, light heavy, and heavy, he fought 106 fights and lost only four of them.

And he lost no more the rest of his life. He worked at a variety of jobs until 1934, when the people of St. Paul asked him to run for Sheriff of Ramsey County. The community was known as a safe haven for gangsters—and Tommy accepted the challenge of cleaning up the community.

He was more than a highly efficient police officer the next 24 years. He was an influence for community betterment, and particularly for youngsters. For instance, the town of Osakis, where he had a farm, needed a new church. Said Tom: "I was lucky to be able to build one when they needed it badly. It was an example to the kids to show them that spiritual values are the most important things in life."

Those same spiritual values inspired Gibbons to his work in the Boy Scout movement. A long-time member of the Board of Directors of the Area Council and the Boy Scout Arch Diocese Committee, he was one of the few adults to be awarded the Order of the Silver Beaver for his contribution to Scouting. A devout church man, he was awarded the Bene Marenti in 1928, the Knight of Gregory Award in 1951.

Yes, Tom Gibbons was more than the man who fought Jack Dempsey at Shelby. He was the Cosmopolitan Club "District Citizen of the year;" a member of the Governor's Youth Conference Commission; Chairman of the National Sheriff's Advisory Commission on Youth—if the organization or the work was for youth, Tom Gibbons was there working.

Small wonder that to the St. Paul Junior Chamber of Commerce—and certainly to his family—he was "Father of the Year!"

Few people remember what happened to other great fighters of history. Sullivan, Kilrain, Corbett, Fitzsimmons, Jack Johnson—what did they do after their brief moments in the lights?

But these men, Dempsey and Gibbons are different. Their improbable meeting was only the beginning of their legend. To the thousands of people who know them personally— and the millions who feel they do—Jack Dempsey and Tom Gibbons are

"Winnahs—and still champions!"

from an early English volume

POPULAR PASTIMES

"The Letting of Humour's Blood in the Head-vaine; with a *New Morisco daunced by seven Satyres upon the bottome of Diogenes' tubbe:"* 8vo, Lond. 1611.

"Man, I dare challenge thee the THROW THE SLEDGE,
To jump or LEAPE over ditch or hedge,
To WRASTLE, play at STOOLEBALL, or to RUNNE:
To PITCH THE BARRE, or to SHOOTE OFF A GUNNE:
To play at LOGGETS, NINE HOLES, or TEN PINNES:
To try it out at FOOTBALL by the shinnes:
At TICKTACKE, IRISH NODDIE, MAW, and RUFFE,
At HOT-COCKLES, LEAP-FROG, or BLINDMAN-BUFFE;
To drink halfe-pots, or deale at the whole can:
To play at BASE, or PEN-AND-YNKHORNE SIR JHAN;
To daunce the MORRIS, play at BARLEY-BREAKE,
At all exploytes a man can thinke or speake;
At SHOVE-GROATE, VENTER-POYNT, or CROSSE & PILE,
At BESHROW HIM THAT'S LAST AT YONDER STYLE;
At LEAPING O'ER A MIDSOMMER-BON-FIER,
Or at the DRAWING DUN OUT OF THE MYER:
At any of those, or all these presently,
Wagge but your finger, I am for you, I!"

This is a sport which makes the body's
very liver curl with enjoyment.

—MARK TWAIN, *Life on the Mississippi.*

MAY DAY

This is peculiarly an English floral festival, and one observed for centuries among the rural population of "Merrie England." It is on the threshold of summer in the southern countries, and the hawthorn bush, popularly known as "The May," is usually in full bloom. In some parts of the island the young men go out very early to the woods, singing this quaint old song:—

> "Come, lads, with your bills,
>   To the woods we'll away,
>   We'll gather the boughs,
>   And we'll celebrate May.
>
> "We'll bring our load home,
>   As we've oft done before,
>   And leave a green bough
>   At each pretty maid's door."

The May-pole, garlanded with flowers, and around which the village revels were held, was an important feature in English rustic life for hundreds of years, and is yet in some secluded corners. In some places the children and young women go about early in the morning hanging green boughs to the doors, singing this song, with variations.

STEPHEN A. DOUGLAS—"LITTLE GIANT"

For ten years he lived in Springfield and, despite his diminutive size, was one of its conspicuous figures. He even profited by the contrast that he presented to these other giants in the earth who made up the General Assembly. For they amiably decided that with his self-confidence, his leonine head, and his knack of getting on, he must be a giant in his own way. And a "little giant," as Douglas came to be called, is a better object of public adulation than an ordinary giant, especially when six feet of manhood is the routine rule.

During the time Lincoln was becoming engaged to Mary Todd, suffering the torments of doubt, parting from her and coming back again, Stephen was resolutely getting on. He went to all the parties. Three or four times a week the great ones of the community entertained, striving always to maintain the standards set by the aristocratic Ninian Edwards. Douglas danced under the generous glow of candlelight and flattered Mary Todd. Once, when she had been the subject of audacious conversation, Mary responded to the question of whether she would rather marry Lincoln or Douglas by saying that she would much prefer the one who had the better chance of being president.

But there was never any doubt in her strange mind as to which that would be. For Mary Todd had the neurotic's gift of insight. Stephen Douglas had become a fastidious and worldly gallant of the kind she had known in Kentucky. He dressed well. He was good at small talk and possessed all the social graces, but still Mary Todd continued to prefer her restless reluctant lover, Abe Lincoln. Gossip has tried hard to prove that there was romantic rivalry between Lincoln and Douglas before there was political rivalry. But the most industrious efforts display a poor little stock of sentimental melodrama. Mary Todd flirted no more with Douglas than high-spirited girls in worldly societies have always permitted themselves to flirt with eligible, responsive bachelors.

Douglas's interest was quite as lightly engaged. His preoccupations were never with women, though he married twice. He cared first for himself; second, for the lovely abstract idea of power; third, for the Democratic party through which he proposed to become a leader.

He succeeded in almost everything that he attempted. Having been a judge of the supreme court in his own state, the next inevitable step in his progress was to take over the field of national politics as a United States senator. Indulgent Illinois advanced him to that post at an amazingly early age.

She became a legend in the minds of the people who had given him these extraordinary opportunities. He was always audacious, always confident. His speeches before the United States Senate made him a noticeable figure. Not all the attention that he drew was friendly. John Quincy Adams, of Massachusetts, quite inevitably thought him a noisy, bombastic, and rather absurd person. But most of the rest of the world did not agree. Two beautiful women did not.

The first of these was Martha Martin, daughter of a North Carolina planter through whom he came in contact with the art of gracious living. She gave him two children, a set of friends whose attitudes were those dictated by the southern economy, and a superior degree of worldly comfort. When she died he became responsible for her property, which included 150 slaves.

After a period of widowhood, during which he was distinctly less the fastidious worldling and distinctly more the whisky drinker, Douglas married again. The second match was more brilliant than the first. Adele Cutts was the equivalent of the much-publicized glamour girl of our own day. Indeed, the papers swooned into fatuity with much more abandon than any publication today could master. The Washington *Post*, reporting the wedding, detailed her charms at length, concluding with this verbal sunburst: "On her clear, peachy complexion, there is a perpetual war of the roses—the red and the white—each failing to maintain sole supremacy."

She was hardly more than half Douglas's age. Her distinguished background was revered in Washington society, which had not forgotten her delightful great-aunt, Dolly Madison. She could have married anyone. She chose Stephen Douglas.

How's for a little game

There are few who sit down to a quiet rubber that are aware of the possible combinations of the pack of fifty-two cards. As a curious fact, not found in Hoyle, it is worth recording here, that the possible combinations of a pack of cards cannot be numerically represented by less than forty-seven figures, arrayed in the following order:
16, 250, 563, 659, 176, 029, 962, 568, 164, 794, 000, 749, 006, 367, 006, 400.

An old work on card-playing sums up the morality of the practice, very concisely, in the following lines:
' He who hopes at cards to win,
Must never think that cheating 's sin;
To make a trick whene'er he can,
No matter how, should be the plan.
No case of conscience must he make,
Except how he may save his stake;
The only object of his prayers
Not to be caught and kicked down stairs.'

A more summary process of ejectment, even, than kicking down stairs, seems to have been occasionally adopted in the olden time; sharpers having sometimes been thrown out of a window. A person so served at Bath, it is said, went to a solicitor for advice, when the following conversation took place:
' Says the lawyer: "What motive for treatment so hard?"
"Dear sir, all my crime was but—slipping a card."

Cards were at first for benefit designed,
Sent to amuse, not to enslave the mind.

—DAVID GARRICK.

Great Adventure but two near tragedies

Towards evening the men in the hindmost canoes discovered a large brown bear; . . . six of them, all good hunters, . . . concealing themselves by a small eminence came unperceived within forty paces of him. Four of the hunters now fired, and each lodged a ball in his body, two of them directly through the lungs. The furious animal sprang up and ran open-mouthed upon them; as he came near, the two hunters who had reserved their fire gave him two wounds, one of which, breaking his shoulder, retarded his motion for a moment; but before they could reload he was so near that they were obliged to run to the river. . . . Two jumped into the canoe; the other four separated, and concealing themselves in the willows fired as fast as each could reload. . . . At last he [the bear] pursued two of them so closely that they threw aside their guns and pouches and jumped down a perpendicular bank of twenty feet into the river. The bear sprang after them, and was within a few feet of the hindmost when one of the hunters on shore shot him in the head and finally killed him; they dragged him to the shore, and found that eight balls had passed through him in different directions. . . .

At camp . . . we had been as much terrified by an accident of a different kind. This was the narrow escape of one of our canoes containing all our papers, instruments, medicine, and almost every article indispensable for the success of our enterprise. The canoe being under sail, a sudden squall of wind struck her obliquely and turned her considerably. The man at the helm, who was unluckily the worst steersman of the party, became alarmed, and instead of putting her before the wind luffed her up into it. The wind was so high that it forced the brace of the square-sail out of the hand of the man who was attending it, and instantly upset the canoe, which would have been turned bottom upward but for the resistance made by the awning. Such was the confusion on board, and the waves ran so high, that it was half a minute before she righted, and then [was] nearly full of water; but by baling out she was kept from sinking until they rowed ashore. Besides the loss of the lives of three men who, not being able to swim, would probably have perished, we should have been deprived of nearly everything necessary for our purposes, at a distance of between two and three thousand miles from any place where we could supply the deficiency.

THE IDEAL HUSBAND TO HIS WIFE

We've lived for forty years, dear wife,
    And walked together side by side,
And you today are just as dear
    As when you were my bride.
I've tried to make life glad for you,
    One long, sweet honeymoon of joy,
A dream of marital content,
    Without the least alloy.
I've smoothed all boulders from our path,
    That we in peace might toil along,
But always hastening to admit
    That I was right and you were wrong.

No mad diversity of creed
    Has ever sundered me from thee;
For I permit you evermore
    To borrow your ideas of me.
And thus it is, through weal or woe,
    Our love forevermore endures;
For I permit that you should take
    My views and creeds, and make them yours.
And thus I let you have my way,
    And thus in peace we toil along,
For I am willing to admit
    That I am right and you are wrong.

THE EDITOR'S STRATEGY

A certain Western town was infested by gamblers, whose presence was a source of annoyance to the citizens, who told the editor that if he did not come out against the offenders they would not patronize his paper. He replied that he would give them a "smasher" next day. Sure enough, his next issue contained the promised "smasher"; and on the following morning the redoubtable editor was seated in his sanctum, when in walked a large man, with a club in his hand, who demanded to know if the editor was in. "No, sir," was the reply; "he has stepped out. Take a seat and read the papers—he will return in a minute." Down sat the indignant man of cards, crossed his legs, with his club between them, and commenced reading a paper. In the meantime the editor quietly went downstairs, and at the landing he met another excited man, with a cudgel in his hand, who asked if the editor was in. "Yes, sir," was the prompt response; "you'll find him seated upstairs, reading a newspaper." This individual, on entering the room, with a furious oath began a violent assault upon the first avenger, which was resisted with equal ferocity, and a very pretty battle ensued, followed by mutual explanations and alliance, offensive and defensive, against the common enemy.

DRAW-POKER

Four men were playing "solo whist." One was cheating and had only one eye. Another of the party saw him cheat; he drew a revolver and placed it on the table, saying: "The first man I catch cheating I'll shoot his other eye out."

LAWYER'S DAUGHTER

"To me, I swear, you're a volume rare—"
But she said with judicial look,
"Your oath's not valid at Common Law
Until you've kissed the Book."

J. H. THACHER

THE LAWYER'S INVOCATION TO SPRING

Whereas, on certain boughs and sprays
Now divers birds are heard to sing,
And sundry flowers their heads upraise,
Hail to the coming on of Spring!

The songs of those said birds arouse
The memory of our youthful hours,
As green as those said sprays and boughs,
As fresh and sweet as those said flowers.

The birds aforesaid—happy pairs—
Love, 'mid the aforesaid boughs, inshrines
In freehold nests; themselves their heirs,
Administrators, and assigns.

O busiest term of Cupid's Court,
Where tender plaintiff's actions bring,—
Season of frolic and of sport,
Hail, as aforesaid, coming Spring!

HENRY HOWARD BROWNELL

SAUNA

by John C. Frohlicher

Strictly for Those Who Like Their
Coffee Inky Black and Beans Thick With Molasses

We've driven 250 miles, and cut a hole in the ice to take the first bath of spring. Minnesota's winter still shows its claws and spits like a lynx-cat in a trap, but that bath is almost ritual. And a bath in a Finnish sauna, on the shore of a wilderness lake, is something that releases the spirit as well as the body from the clamps of too-long cold.

The steam bath is the first structure a good Finn builds when he moves to a new country. While our host and his brothers, the Koskis, were born in Ely, they are nevertheless good Finns. Their sauna, at the summer place on Burntside Lake, is good, too.

Basically it's a big airtight stove covered with boulders as big as your two fists, set in the back room of a two-room cabin. Three tiers of seats rise like small bleachers to near the roof, where a ventilator opens and closes as a lever is moved. An open-ended barrel stands near the stove, connected with a coil of pipe. A pump provides water—when the frost isn't nine feet down. Now water is pailed from the hole through the ice mentioned earlier at the end of the drifted-in dock. The water is about three feet deep.

But this is mechanics. Taking a sauna is almost a ceremony—set by custom and practice. We men leave the house right after breakfast. The women are already discussing AAUW activities, for our hostess is State President of the American Association of University Women, and preparing for the afternoon meal, to be eaten at the lake. But that's women's work.

So we stop at the store for candy bars and butter, and at the clothier's for "chopper" mitts and a pair of "tausas." These are hand-made felt socks that stop any cold right at the rubber of a man's footgear, and are mighty necessary in the below-zero temperatures woodsmen often fight. The drive to the lake is leisurely—a stop at the bridge to look for muskrat or beaver activity; a remark at trails made by deer crossing from the swamps; a moment or so watching a flock of juncos working a weed bed; a silent appreciation of bright sunlight shattering on frost-furred trees.

The cabin sits on a jackpine covered shelf about fifty feet above the lake, while the sauna is right at the shore about 200 yards away. The trail is icy and the footing bad, but we slip down it. Two more Koski men are already here—for a sauna is a family affair. Walter stops his chopping and puts out a hard hand. "Spring soon" he says. "Last week, a robin. Today, a city feller!"

Across the white lake a car speeds, a snow cloud trailing it where a tree drags, branches and all. It was felled by beaver miles up the shore. The tender bark was eaten, and Arvo Koski hauls in the carcass for sauna wood. By car in winter and by boat in summer these men gather fuel for that sauna, and the split and neatly-piled stack of birch, popple and balm of gilead are kept high.

The sauna fire is going, has been since sunup. It takes a long time to get those rocks so hot that water steams off them as fast as it is tossed on, but there's much to be done. The canoes, racked in the boathouse, are checked casually. A new bucksaw frame, whittled on the spot, must be inspected and tried. The cross-cut saw needs dragging and the axe needs swinging. The Koskis need their amusement at the clumsiness of the "city feller," too! A fast trip has to be made to a cedar swamp across the lake, where we dig under drifts for twigs that are emarald green, not burned brown by frost. We bind the twigs into whiskbroom like bundles, to be used as switches during the bath.

Cars stop at the top of the hill, park along the highway. The women come sliding down the trail, bright as cardinals and bluejays in their winter coats. Men bring the baskets and kettles down—part of the ritual of this sauna is the meal, heated and even cooked in part over an open fire, eaten with snowbanks deep around us.

There's a jabber of greetings and comment as the five women go into the sauna, where the roof is black from melted snow and steam is drifting from the ventilator. Arvo piles some finely-cut wood around a curl of birchbark at the shore fireplace and touches a lighted match to it. The flames curl high, and he goes to the water hole to fill the coffee pot.

> *I fly to the hot baths, there you din my ears;*
> *I seek the cold bath, there I cannot swim for*
> *your noise.*
>   —MARTIAL, EPIGRAMS.

Finn coffee is different. It's a standard brand, to begin with. But when it is compounded of northwoods lake water, amber from muskeg and the iron of the rocks and perhaps a least whisper of ash and charcoal, and then brought to a boil three times—then it is something to remember. We sit on chunks of wood pulled around the blaze. We watch a red squirrel get up nerve to approach the heap of food containers. He's an old-timer on his lake and knows what they mean.

An hour goes by. There are shrieks of laughter from the sauna as the women splash each other with cold water—and then they come out, bright kerchiefs around each head. We men move in and peel our heavy clothing, put on bathing trunks. None of this cold water splashing inside the sauna for us!

Into the stove room and a seat on the lowest bench, where the heat isn't so intense. Emil tosses a cup of water on the hot stones. It hisses away with barely a trace of steam. The air is saturated with moisture, and the sweat begins to run as pores open. Under urging, we move up to the top bench, where we soon gasp in what seems like concentrated flame.

We sluice warm water from the barrel over our shoulders, rub soap, wipe the salt sweat from our eyes. The water drains through a hole in the floor, forms strange shapes as it goes toward the lake level.

This is old, this type of bathing. The Finns practiced it countless generations ago. Viking warriors stood amazed at the pretentious marble steam baths they saw in ravaged Rome. A boyhood memory comes back—of a low skin lodge hidden in a fold of the high Montana plains; of hot rocks and water whisked on them from a buffalo tail; of a Black-foot medicine man singing a chant outside the lodge where two young boys, Indian and white, are purified for their manhood rites.

Almost broiled, we dash through the dressing room, out the door and down the dock. We step through the hole in the ice—up to our waists in the frigid water. "Way under!" yell the Finns, and we hear the woman laugh as we come up and out, scrambling for the dock and the warmth of the dressing room.

Hercules, how cold is this bath of yours?

Once again we enter the heat, this time switching ourselves with the cedar whips. Then into the lake—and out, tingling all over, buoyant as youngsters and clean as—well, clean as a well-saunaed Finn.

There's nothing cuts the winter's bonds like a sauna. Nothing snaps tensions like the plunge almost beneath the ice.

At the fireplace a "moyuka" is teaming. This is fish chowder whose base is a big trout, frozen in the ice on the lake since spearing season closed. It's a good food. There's homemade bread, baked according to an old mother-to-daughter recipe, crusty and dripping butter. Baked beans, flavored with crisp pork cubes and rich with molasses. Coffee. More coffee as we empty the barrel in the sauna, clean the place up and carry the baskets back to the cars. The women leave for town.

We don't talk much around the fire. We watch the sun drop behind the low, rounded hills of the Mesabi and Vermillion ranges; we watch the trees turn black across the lake. Through the first dusk comes a long, far-distant howl, almost a song. "Wolf" we mutter as we start toward home.

They who bathe in May will soon be laid in clay;
They who bathe in June will sing a merry tune;
They who bathe in July will dance like a fly.

—HONE'S, *Table-Book.*

Let the great winds their worst and wildest blow,
Of the gold weather round us mellow slow;
We have fulfilled ourselves, and we can dare,
And we can conquer, though we may not share
In the rich quiet of the after-glow,
What is to come.
—W. E. HENLEY

Be discreet in all things, and so render it unnecessary to be mysterious about any.
— DUKE OF WELLINGTON

SOUP

by
CARL SANDBURG
from Smoke and Steel

I saw a famous man eating soup.
I say he was lifting a fat broth
Into his mouth with a spoon.
His name was in the newspapers that day
Spelled out in tall black headlines
And thousands of people were talking about him.

When I saw him,
He sat bending his head over a plate
Putting soup in his mouth with a spoon.

TAWNY

by
CARL SANDBURG
from Smoke and Steel

These are the tawny days: your face comes back.

The grapes take on purple: the sunsets redden early on the trellis.

The bashful mornings hurl gray mist on the stripes of sunrise.

Creep, silver on the field, the frost is welcome.

Run on, yellow balls on the hills, and you tawny pumpkin flowers, chasing your lines of orange.

Tawny days: and your face again.

A MELONAIRE POET

MISS AMY LOWELL in September *Dial*

I am joyful because of my melons,
I am joyful because of my beans,
I am joyful because of my squashes.

A KNIGHT'S CREED

from Idylls of the King
by ALFRED LORD TENNYSON

But I was first of all the kings who drew
The knighthood-errant of this realm and all
The realms together under me, their Head,
In that fair Order of my Table Round,
A glorious company, the flower of men,
To serve as model for the mighty world,
And be the fair beginning of a time.
I made them lay their hands in mine and swear
To reverence the King, as if he were
Their conscience, and their conscience as their King,
To break the heathen and uphold the Christ,
To ride abroad redressing human wrongs,
To speak no slander, no, nor listen to it,
To honor his own word as if his God's,
To lead sweet lives in purest chastity,
To love one maiden only, cleave to her,
And worship her by years of noble deeds,
Until they won her; for indeed I knew
Of no more subtle master under heaven
Than is the maiden passion for a maid,
Not only to keep down the base in man,
But teach high thought, and amiable words
And courtliness, and the desire of fame,
And love of truth, and all that makes a man.

Knighthood, of all the prerogatives that men enjoy,
the antiquity of noblesse, is the first and greatest; it is
above ranks and dignities, above the gift of kings,
who can only give birth to it; only the duration of
time, the course of centuries, constitutes its honor and
glory.

                                        History of Phillip

JESSIE

Jessie is both young and fair,
Dewy eyes and sunny hair;
Sunny hair and dewy eyes
Are not where her beauty lies.

Jessie is both kind and true,
Heart of gold and will of yew;
Will of yew and heart of gold —
Still her charms are scarcely told.

If she yet remain unsung,
Pretty, constant, docile, young.
What remains not here compiled?
Jessie is a little child!

— BRET HARTE

*Lo children are a heritage of the Lord: and the fruit of
the womb is his reward. As arrows are in the hand of a
mighty man; so are children of the youth. Happy is the
man that hath his quiver full of them.*

—PSALMS 128, 3-5

*Ah! What would the world be to us
If the children were no more?
We should dread the desert behind us
Worse than the dark before.*

—LONGFELLOW, *Children*

*O blessed vision! happy child!
Thou art so exquisitely wild,
I think of thee with many fears
For what may be thy lot in future years.*

—WORDSWORTH, *To Hartley Coleridge, age 6*

A PAIR OF DICE

We are little brethren twain,
Arbiters of loss and gain.
Many to our counters run,
Some are made and some undone:
But men find it to their cost,
Few are made, but numbers lost.
Though we play them tricks for ever,
Yet they always hope our favor.

Shake off the shackles of this tyrant vice;
Hear other calls than those of cards and dice;
Be learn'd in nobler arts than arts of play;
And other debts than those of honor pay.

—DAVID GARRICK, The Gamester

"But the strawberry-roan, with the sharp backbone"
OVER THE WEST HILLS

SHE has tightened her cinch by another inch,
    she has shortened her stirrup-strap,
And she's off with a whirl of horse and girl,
    and I'm a lucky chap!

With a "Catch if you can! I'm as good as a man!"
    at a breakneck pace we ride.
I have all but placed my arm round her waist,
    as we gallop side by side.

When "Roop! Ki Yi!!" and her elbows high,
    she spurts in the cowboy style:
With a jerk and a saw at her horse's jaw,
    she's ahead for another mile!

And it's Nancy's dust that breathe I must,
    and it's Nancy's trail I follow,
Till I leave the rut for a steep short-cut,
    and I've caught her down in the hollow.

Then into the creek, with a splash and a shriek,
    to her saddle-girth she dares;
"Oh, make for the shoal, or he'll stop and roll!"
    But it's little that Nancy cares.

And up the hill she's ahead of me still,
    and over the ridge we go!
And my steaming nag has begun to lag;
    but it isn't my fault, I know.

Oh! fair astride does Nancy ride,
    and her spur she uses free,
And it's little she cares for the gown she wears,
    and it's little she cares for me!

But the strawberry-roan, with the sharp backbone,
    that Nancy rode that day,
He doesn't forget that Saturday yet
    when Nancy led the way!

A RONDELAY

MAN is for woman made
   And woman made for man:
As the spur is for the jade,
As the scabbard for the blade,
   As for liquor is the can,
So man's for woman made,
   And woman made for man.

As the sceptre to be sway'd,
As to-night the serenade,
   As for pudding in the pan,
   As to cool us is the fan,
So man's for woman made,

   And woman made for man.
Be she widow, wife, or maid,
Be she wanton, be she staid,
Be she well or ill array'd

So man's for woman made.
   And woman made for man.

      — PETER ANTHONY MOTTEUX
      (1660-1718)

TIT FOR TAT

If I kiss you, do you find
   Wrong and outrage in it?
You may punish me in kind;
   Kiss me then this minute.

      — STRATO

THE BIRTH OF PLEASURE
by PERCY B. SHELLEY
Date, 1819. Published by Garnett, 1862.

At the creation of the Earth
Pleasure, that divinest birth,
From the soil of Heaven did rise,
Wrapped in sweet wild melodies —
Like an exhalation wreathing
To the sound of air low-breathing
Through Æolian pines, which make
A shade and shelter to the lake
Whence it rises soft and slow;
Her life-breathing [limbs] did flow
In the harmony divine
Of an ever-lengthening line
Which enwrapped her perfect form
With a beauty clear and warm.

*When we say, then, that pleasure is the end and aim of
life, we do not mean the pleasures of the prodigal or the
pleasures of sensuality. . . . By pleasure we mean the
absence of pain in the body and of trouble in the soul.*
—EPICURUS

*The pleasure of life is according to the man that lives it,
and not according to the work or place.*
—EMERSON, *Fate*

*In life there is nothing more unexpected and surprising
than the arrivals and departures of pleasure. If we find it
in one place today, it is vain to seek it there tomorrow.
You cannot lay a trap for it.*
—ALEXANDER SMITH, *City Poem: A Boy's Dream*

*Pleasure is the rock which most young people spit upon:
they launch out with crowded sails in quest of it, but without a compass to direct their course, or reason sufficient
to steer the vessel.*
—LORD CHESTERFIELD, *Letters*

*Pleasure is "the bait of sin" because men are caught
thereon like fish on a worm.*
—PLATO

LIVE FOR A GOAL

There is one feature that is always prominent in those who are strong personalities, and that is a unity of purpose, a concentration of mind, a fixed determination which pursues its object steadily and without wavering. Whether it be a statesman, a general, a merchant, or a minister of God, they are all alike in this, that their motto is that of St. Paul, "One thing I do." And this unity of purpose is what religious people call consecration. It is the separation of one duty, one ambition, one resolve from all others, and giving it the prominent place in the life. It is the application to human life of that which is often done with buildings, vessels, and the like.—*The Reverend G. H. S. Walpole*, "Personality and Power."

The secret of success is concentration: wherever there has been a great life, or a great work, that has gone before. Taste everything a little, look at everything a little; but live for one thing. Anything is possible to a man who knows his end, and moves straight for it, and for it alone.—*Ralph Iron.*

The one prudence in life is concentration; the one evil is dissipation; and it makes no difference whether our dissipations are coarse or fine . . . Everything is good which takes away one plaything and delusion more, and drives us home to add one stroke of faithful work. — EMERSON, *Conduct of Life.*

It is said—

That there is hardly a bar of his music which Beethoven did not rewrite a dozen times.

That Bryant rewrote "Thanatopsis" a hundred times.

That Gibbon rewrote his *Autobiography* nine times.

That Plato wrote the first sentence in his *Republic* nine times.

That Vergil spent twelve years writing his *Aeneid.*

JUST KEEP RINGING THAT PHONE

by AL CAPP

I make it a point never to keep a President of the United States waiting no matter how much it may inconvenience me.

And so I once arrived at the Mayflower Hotel before Mr. Eisenhower had asked me (and several hundred others) to a conference at the White House.

As I was shown into the living room of my suite, I noticed that door was numbered 456, and my bedroom door, adjoining, was marked 456-A.

I called the phone operator and said, "I must be awakened by 8 o'clock tomorrow morning. I have an appointment at the White House at 10."

"I'll ring you at 8 o'clock," she said, "that's all?"

* * *

"NO," I said. "I'm a stubborn sleeper, And I'm tricky.

"I need protection against myself. When you ring me I'll say 'Getting right up.' Don't let that fool you. I'll go right back to sleep. So ring me again at 8:02, again at 8:04, again at 8:06. In fact, ring me every two minutes, for a full hour. Disregard any promises I make to get up, my pleas for mercy, any abusive language or threats. Just keep ringing that phone.

"Keep ringing the phone, irregardless. Got it! Anything else?"

"Yes, I said. Don't ring 456. That phone is in my living room, far enough away so that I can survive the racket. Ring the phone in 456-A. That one's next to my bed. It'll drive me crazy."

"Drive you crazy. Got it," said the girl. "Good night."

* * *

I THEN called Room Service. I ordered bacon and

eggs, buckwheat cakes and maple sirup, German saus-
ages, Danish pastry, English muffins, French crullers
and coffee.

"*Anything else?*" *asked Room Service.*

"*Yes,*" *I said.* "*Have the whole mess at my door at 8
sharp. If I don't answer the waiter's knock, which I
won't, I authorize you to give him a key. Tell him to
push the table in, and leave it alongside my bed, under
my nose. The maddening aroma of all those goodies will
make it impossible for me to go on sleeping.*"

Then I turned in, serene in the knowledge that I had
done everything any redblooded American could do to
make sure he would not fail his President.

* * *

NEXT MORNING I was awakened by the ringing
of my phone. I left refreshed. And small wonder. It was
12 o'clock, the White House conference was over, and it
was the State Department calling wanting to know
where in hell I'd been.

Raging, I called the hotel manager.

*I told him I intended to tear down his hotel with my
bare hands. I told him of the infinite precautions I had
taken the night before, the detailed instructions to the
phone operator, the fantastic order to Room Service,
the final cunning strategy of ordering the entire spectacle to be staged in my bedroom, 456-A.*

"Before you tear the Mayflower down," he said, "will
you step into the corridor with me." Still roaring, I did.

* * *

HE KNOCKED at 456-A. A man opened the door.
He looked terrible. 456-A wasn't my bedroom.

"*I have had one hell of a night,*" *said the man.*
"*Name's Bowman, from Texas. Finished my business in*

Washington last night and sorta celebrated. Got in at six. I didn't care. I could sleep all day."

He moaned.

"I'd hardly closed my eyes when the phone starts ringing. Some crazy woman tells me I gotta get up. I say, 'Lady, the hell I will' and hang up. Two minutes later she phones again. And again—and again!!! You wouldn't believe it, but she just wouldn't stop."

"I believe it," I said.

" 'YOU RING ONCE MORE,' I yells at this LUNA-TIC," continued Mr. Bowman, "AND I'LL RIP THE PHONE OUT!' "

"Two minutes later she rings again. I rip the phone out.

"I begin to crawl back to bed—and ANOTHER lunatic begins hammering at my door. This one's a man. I tell him to stop. He won't stop. He yells 'OPEN THAT DOOR.' I won't open the door!! So HE opens the door and wheels in the craziest breakfast you ever saw!"

I'd rather have Fingers than Toes;
I'd rather have Ears than a Nose!
  And as for my Hair,
  I'm glad it's all there,
I'll be awfully sad when it goes!

Like the measles, love is most dangerous when it comes late in life.
— LORD BYRON

THE RAINY DAY.

The day is cold and dark and dreary;
It rains, and the wind is never weary;
The vine still clings to the mouldering wall,
But at every gust the dead leaves fall:
    And the day is dark and dreary.

My life is cold, and dark, and dreary;
It rains, and the wind is never weary;
My thoughts still cling to the mouldering past,
But the hopes of youth fall thick in the blast,
    And the days are dark and dreary.

Be still, sad heart; and cease repining;
Behind the clouds is the sun still shining;
Thy fate is the common fate of all;
Into each life some rain must fall,
    Some days must be dark and dreary.

—HENRY WADSWORTH LONGFELLOW.

LOW SPIRITS

If your spirits are low, do something; if you have been doing something, do something different.—E. E. Hall.

There is always sunshine, only we must do our part: we must move into it.—C. L. Burnham.

It is the lifted face that feels the shining of the sun.—Browning.

The cure of heart-ache is to be found in occupations which take us away from our petty self-regardings, our self-pityings, our morbid broodings, and which connect our life with other lives and with other affairs, or merge our individual interest in the larger whole.—C. G. Ames.

"The Rain is Over and Gone"

The Cock is crowing,
The stream is flowing,
The small birds twitter,
The lake doth glitter,
The green field sleeps in the sun;
The oldest and youngest
Are at work with the strongest;
The cattle are grazing,
Their heads never raising;
There are forty feeding like one!

Like an army defeated
The snow hath retreated,
And now doth fare ill
On the top of the bare hill;
The ploughboy is whooping—anon—anon:
There's joy in the mountains;
There's life in the fountains;
Small clouds are sailing,
Blue sky prevailing;
The rain is over and gone!

WORDSWORTH.

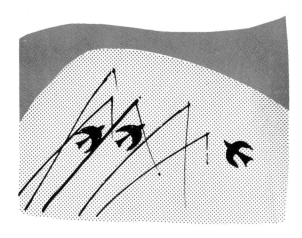

Time is a young man with ball player legs

by
CARL SANDBURG
from Smoke and Steel

Let it go on; let the love of this hour be poured out till all the answers are made, the last dollar spent and the last blood gone.

Time runs with an ax and a hammer, time slides down the hallways with a pass-key and a master-key and time gets by, time wins.

Let the love of this hour go on; let all the oaths and children and people of this love be clean as a washed stone under a waterfall in the sun.

Time is a young man with ballplayer legs, time runs a winning race against life and the clocks, time tickles with rust and spots.

Let love go on; the heartbeats are measured out with a measuring glass, so many apiece to gamble with, to use and spend and reckon; let love go on.

WHAT IS LOVE?

Ask not of me, love, what is love?
Ask what is good of God above—
Ask of the great sun what is light—
Ask what is darkness of the night—
Ask sin of what may be forgiven—
Ask what is happiness of Heaven—
Ask what is folly of the crowd—
Ask what is fashion of the shroud—
Ask what is sweetness of thy kiss—
Ask of thyself what beauty is.

—P. J. BAILEY, *Festus.*

BALLADE OF DREAMS TRANSPOSED
"The luck of the rover's the thing for me"

SOME may like to be shut in a cage,
 Cooped in a corner, a-tippling tea,
Some may in troublesome toil engage;
  But the luck of a rover 's the thing for me!
  Over the mountain and over the sea,
Now in the country and now in the town,
  And when I'm wrinkled and withered, maybe
Then I'll marry and settle down.

Some may pore over printed page
 And never know bird, nor beast, nor tree,
Watching the world from book or stage;
  But the luck of a rover 's the thing for me!
  So ho! for the forest, and ho! for the lea,
And ho! for the river and prairie brown,
  And ho! for a gay long jubilee,—
Then I'll marry and settle down.

Why should I wait till gray old age
 Brings me chance to be rich and free?
I have no money—it makes me rage;
  But the luck of a rover 's the thing for me!
  Though oft, with my lover upon my knee
(She has frolicsome eyes and a fetching gown!)
  I fear if my heart 's to be held in fee,—
Then I'll marry and settle down.

Envoy

Prince, my sweetheart will not agree,—
But the luck of a rover 's the thing for me!
She says I must stay, and I fear her frown,—
Then I'll marry and settle down.

GELETT BURGESS

In Flanders Field

In Flanders fields the poppies blow
Between the crosses, row on row,
   That mark our place; and in the sky
   The larks, still bravely singing, fly
Scarce heard amid the guns below.

We are the Dead. Short days ago
We lived, felt dawn, saw sunset glow,
   Loved and were loved, and now we lie,
   In Flanders fields.

Take up our quarrel with the foe:
To you from failing hands we throw
   The torch; be yours to hold it high.
   If ye break faith with us who die
We shall not sleep, though poppies grow
   In Flanders fields.

JOHN McCRAE

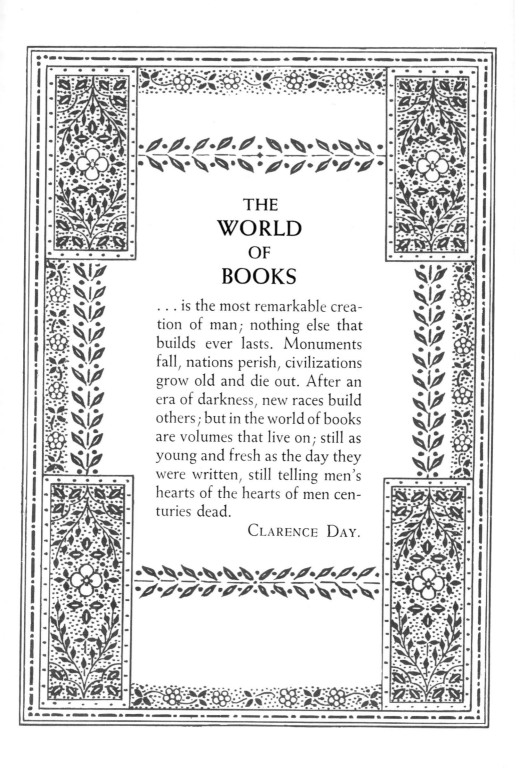

THE
WORLD
OF
BOOKS

... is the most remarkable creation of man; nothing else that builds ever lasts. Monuments fall, nations perish, civilizations grow old and die out. After an era of darkness, new races build others; but in the world of books are volumes that live on; still as young and fresh as the day they were written, still telling men's hearts of the hearts of men centuries dead.

CLARENCE DAY.

First Draft of Declaration of Independence.

We hold these truths to be self-evident, that all men are created equal, that they are endowed by their Creator with certain unalien Rights, that among these are Life, Liberty and the pursuit of Happiness. That to secure these rights, Governments are instituted among Men, deriving their just powers from the consent of the governed. That whenever any Form of Government becomes destructive of these ends, it is the Right of the People to alter or to abolish it, and to institute new Government, laying its foundation on such principles and organizing its powers in such form, as to them shall seem most likely to effect their Safety and Happiness ... We, therefore, ... do ... solemnly publish and declare, That these United Colonies are, and of Right ought to be free and independent States ... And for the support of this Declaration, with a firm reliance on the protection of Divine Providence, We mutually pledge to each other our Lives, our Fortunes, and our sacred Honor.

—THOMAS JEFFERSON.

DEAR LAND OF ALL MY LOVE

Long as thine art shall love true love,
Long as thy science truth shall know,
Long as thine eagle harms no dove,
Long as thy law by law shall grow,
Long as thy God is God above,
Thy brother every man below,
So long, dear land of all my love,
Thy name shall shine, thy fame shall glow.

— SIDNEY LANIER
"The Centennial Ode" (1876)

CLANK YOUR CHAINS

"We cannot all serve our country in the same way; but each does his best, according as God has endowed him." In 1830, as a reason for not taking up arms in the War of Liberation, against France: "How could I take up arms without hatred, and how could I hate without youth?" But he was accused at the time of too great admiration of Napoleon. "Clank your chains!" he said to his countrymen, who were endeavoring to shatter them, "the man is too great for you. You will not break them, but only drive them deeper into your flesh." "National hatred," said Goethe to Eckermann, "is something peculiar: you will always find it strongest and most violent in the lowest degree of culture."

The die was now cast; I had passed the Rubicon. Swim or sink, live or die, survive or perish with my country was my unalterable determination.

—JOHN ADAMS.

General Lee, fond father, loving husband — Ever a Gentleman

"You do not know how much I have missed you and the children, my dear Mary. To be alone in a crowd is very solitary. In the woods, I feel sympathy with the trees and birds, in whose company I take delight, but experience no pleasure in a strange crowd. I hope you are all well and will continue so, and, therefore, must again urge you to be very prudent and careful of those dear children. If I could only get a squeeze at that little fellow, turning up his sweet mouth to 'keese baba!' You must not let him run wild in my absence, and will have to exercise firm authority over all of them. This will not require severity or even strictness, but constant attention and an unwavering course. Mildness and forbearance will strengthen their affection for you, while it will maintain your control over them."

". . . I saw a number of little girls all dressed up in their white frocks and pantalets, their hair plaited and tied up with ribbons, running and chasing each other in all directions. I counted twenty-three nearly the same size. As I drew up my horse to admire the spectacle, a man appeared at the door with the twenty-fourth in his arms.

"'My friend,' said I, 'are all these your children?'

"'Yes,' he said, 'and there are nine more in the house, and this is the youngest.'

"Upon further inquiry, however, I found that they were only temporarily his, and that they were invited to a party at his house. He said, however, he had been admiring them before I came up, and just wished that he had a million of dollars, and that they were all his in reality. I do not think the eldest exceeded seven or eight years old. It was the prettiest sight I have seen in the west, and, perhaps, in my life. . . .

HOW TO ASK AND HAVE

"Oh, 'tis time I should talk to your mother,
    Sweet Mary," says I;
"Oh, don't talk to my mother," says Mary,
    Beginning to cry:
"For my mother says men are deceivers,
    And never, I know, will consent;
She says girls in a hurry to marry,
    At leisure repent."

"Then, suppose I should talk to your father,
    Sweet Mary," says I;
"Oh, don't talk to my father," says Mary,
    Beginning to cry:
"For my father he loves me so dearly,
    He'll never consent I should go;—
If you talk to my father," says Mary,
    "He'll surely say 'No.' "

"Then how shall I get you, my jewel,
    Sweet Mary?" says I;
"If your father and mother's so cruel,
    Most surely I'll die!"
"Oh, never say die, dear," says Mary;
    "A way now to save you I see:
Since my parents are both so contrary,
    You'd better ask *me.*"

SAMUEL LOVER

Questions are never indiscreet.
Answers sometimes are.

—OSCAR WILDE, *An Ideal Husband*

THOS. JEFFERSON'S LETTER OF INSTRUCTION TO CAPTAIN MERIWETHER LEWIS

To Meriwether Lewis, esquire, captain of the first regiment of infantry of the United States of America:

Your situation as secretary of the president of the United States has made you acquainted with the objects of my confidential message of January 18, 1803, to the legislature; you have seen the act they passed, which, though expressed in general terms, was meant to sanction those objects, and you are appointed to carry them into execution.

Instruments for ascertaining, by celestial observations, the geography of the country through which you will pass have been already provided. Light articles for barter and presents among the Indians, arms for your attendants, say for from ten to twelve men, boats, tents, and other travelling apparatus, with ammunition, medicine, surgical instruments, and provisions, you will have prepared, with such aids as the secretary at war can yield in his department; and from him also you will receive authority to engage among our troops, by voluntary agreement, the number of attendants abovementioned, over whom you, as their commanding officer, are invested with all the powers the laws give in such a case. . . .

Your mission has been communicated to the ministers here from France, Spain, and Great Britain, and through them to their governments, and such assurances given them as to its objects as we trust will satisfy them. The country of Louisiana having been ceded by Spain to France, the passport you have from the minister of France, the representative of the present sovereign of the country, will be a protection with all its subjects; and that from the minister of England will entitle you to the friendly aid of any traders of that allegiance with whom you may happen to meet.

The object of your mission is to explore the Missouri River, and such principal streams of it as, by its course and communication with the waters of the Pacific ocean, whether the Columbia, Oregan, Colorado, or any other river, may offer the most direct and practicable water-communication across the continent for the purposes of commerce.

Beginning at the mouth of the Missouri, you will take observations of latitude and longitude at all remarkable points on the river.

The interesting points of the portage between the heads of the Missouri, and of the water offering the best communication with the Pacific ocean, should also be fixed by observation, and the course of that water to the ocean in the same manner as that of the Missouri.

Your observations are to be taken with great pains and accuracy. . . . Several copies of these, as well as of your other notes, should be made at leisure times, and put into the care of the most trustworthy of your attendants to guard, by multiplying them, against the accidental losses to which they will be exposed. A further guard would be that one of these copies be on the cuticular membranes of the paper-birch, as less liable to injury from damp than common paper.

. . . You will therefore endeavor to make yourself acquainted, as far as a diligent pursuit of your journey shall admit, with the names of the nations and their numbers;

The extent and limits of their possessions;

Their relations with other tribes or nations;

Their language, traditions, monuments;

Their ordinary occupations in agriculture, fishing, hunting, war, arts, and the implements for these;

Their food, clothing, and domestic accommodations;

The diseases prevalent among them, and the remedies they use;

Moral and physical circumstances which distinguish them from the tribes we know;

Peculiarities in their laws, customs, and dispositions;

And articles of commerce they may need or furnish, and to what extent.

And . . . it will be useful to acquire what knowledge you can of the state of morality, religion, and information among them. . . .

Other objects worthy of notice will be—

The soil and face of the country, its growth and vegetable productions, especially those not of the United States;

The animals of the country generally, and especially those not known in the United States.

PRESIDENT LINCOLN'S ANSWER
to Critics of His Early Months of Administration

"EXECUTIVE MANSION, April 1, 1861.—Hon. W. H. Seward —My Dear Sir: Since parting with you I have been considering your paper dated this day and entitled 'Some Thoughts for the President's Consideration.' The first proposition in it is, 'We are at the end of a month's administration and yet without a policy, either domestic or foreign.'

"At the beginning of that month in the inaugural I said: 'The power confided to me will be used to hold, occupy and possess the property and places belonging to the Government, and to collect the duties and imports.' This had your distinct approval at the time; and taken in connection with the order I immediately gave General Scott, directing him to employ every means in his power to strengthen and hold the forts, comprises the exact domestic policy you urge, with the single exception that it does not propose to abandon Fort Sumter.

.   .   .   .

"The news received yesterday in regard to Santo Domingo certainly brings a new item within the range of our foreign policy, but up to that time we have been preparing circulars and instructions to ministers and the like, all in perfect harmony, without even a suggestion that we had no foreign policy.

"Upon your closing proposition—that 'Whatever policy we adopt, there must be an energetic prosecution of it. For this purpose it must be somebody's business to pursue and direct it incessantly. Either the President must do it himself, and be all the while active in it, or devolve it upon some member of his Cabinet. Once adopted, debates must end, and all agree and abide.' I remark that if this be done, I must do it. When a general line of policy is adopted, I apprehend there is no danger of its being changed without good reason, or continuing to be a subject of unnecessary debate; still, upon points arising in its progress, I wish, and suppose I am entitled to have, the advice of all the Cabinet. Your obedient servant,

"A. LINCOLN."

A LIFE ON THE OCEAN WAVE

A life on the ocean wave,
  A home on the rolling deep,
Where the scattered waters rave,
  And the winds their revels keep!
Like an eagle caged I pine
  On this dull unchanging shore:
Oh! give me the flashing brine,
  The spray and the tempest's roar!

Once more on the deck I stand
  Of my own swift-gliding craft:
Set sail! farewell to the land!
  The gale follows fair abaft.
We shoot through the sparkling foam
  Like an ocean-bird set free;—
Like the ocean-bird, our home
  We'll find far out on the sea.

The land is no longer in view,
  The clouds have begun to frown;
But with a stout vessel and crew,
  We'll say let the storm come down!
And the song of our hearts shall be,
  While the winds and the waters rave,
A home on the rolling sea!
  A life on the ocean wave.

— EPES SARGENT

And I have loved thee, Ocean! And my joy
of youthful sports was on thy breast to be
Borne, like thy bubbles onward. From a boy
I wanton'd with thy breakers, . . .
And trusted to thy billows far and near,
And laid my hand upon thy mane — as I do here.

—BYRON, *Childe Harold*

"NEW FEET WITHIN MY GARDEN GO"

New feet within my garden go,
   New fingers stir the sod;
A troubadour upon the elm
   Betrays the solitude.

New children play upon the green,
   New weary sleep below;
And still the pensive spring returns,
   And still the punctual snow!

THE BEE

Like trains of cars on tracks of plush
   I hear the level bee;
A jar across the flowers goes,
   Their velvet masonry.

Withstands until the sweet assault
   Their chivalry consumes,
While he, victorious, tilts away
   To vanquish other blooms.

His feet are shod with gauze,
   His helmet is of gold;
His breast, a single onyx
   With chrysoprase, inlaid.

His labor is a chant,
   His idleness a tune;
Oh, for a bee's experience
   Of clovers and of noon!

Both from Poems by EMILY DICKINSON

There is no limit to your endurance

We hold that happenings which may even compel the heart to break cannot break the human spirit, or rob it of its most essential qualities. They can rob the body. Bacteria invisible to the naked eye can wear out the body's endurance. They can turn it into a workshop for the manufacture of physical agony, or they can steep nerves and brain in unconsciousness. But there is no such limit to the endurance of the soul—it has access to springs of peace and fortitude which the body cannot reach. Souls within bodies are like dwellers in a wave-washed city, besieged by land but not by sea. And the city may be taken, but its inhabitants, with all that is worth transport, will have embarked already on some glorious fresh adventure, banners flying and sails set.
—MAY KENDALL

Of all things which a man has, next to the Gods,
his soul is the most divine, and most truly his own.
—PLATO, Laws

The soul of man is like the rolling world,
One half in day, the other dipt in night;
The one has music and the flying cloud,
The other, silence and the wakeful stars.
—ALEXANDER SMITH, Horton

It is the soul, and not the strong-box,
which should be filled.
—SENECA

It is much more necessary to cure the soul than
the body, for death is better than a bad life.
—EPICTETUS

THE DOG AND THIEF. 1726.

QUOTH the thief to the dog, let me into your door,
  And I'll give you these delicate bits.
Quoth the dog, I shall then be more villain than you're,
  And besides must be out of my wits.
Your delicate bits will not serve me a meal,
  But my master each day gives me bread;
You'll fly when you get what you came here to steal,
  And I must be hang'd in your stead.

ON THE MOON

I WITH borrow'd silver shine;
What you see is none of mine.
First I show you but a quarter,
Like the bow that guards the Tartar
Then the half, and then the whole,
Ever dancing round the pole.
And what will raise your admiration,
I am not one of God's creation,
But sprung, (and I this truth maintain,)
Like Pallas, from my father's brain.
And after all, I chiefly owe
My beauty to the shades below.
Most wondrous forms you see me wear,
A man, a woman, lion, bear,
A fish, a fowl, a cloud, a field,
All figures heaven or earth can yield;
Like Daphne sometimes in a tree;
Yet am not one of all you see.

ON A CIRCLE

I'M up and down and round about,
Yet all the world can't find me out;
Though hundreds have employ'd their leisure,
They never yet could find my measure.
I'm found almost in every garden,
Nay, in the compass of a farthing.
There's neither chariot, coach, nor mill,
Can move an inch except I will.

ON TIME

Ever eating, never cloying,
All-devouring, all-destroying,
Never finding full repast,
Till I eat the world at last.

ON THE VOWELS

We are little airy creatures,
All of different voice and features;
One of us in glass is set,
One of us you'll find in jet;
T'other you may see in tin,
And the fourth a box within;
If the fifth you should pursue,
It can never fly from you.

ON SNOW

From heaven I fall, though from earth I begin;
No lady alive can show such a skin.
I'm bright as an angel, and light as a feather,
But heavy and dark when you squeeze me together.
Though candour and truth in my aspect I bear,
Yet many poor creatures I help to ensnare.
Though so much of heaven appears in my make,
The foulest impressions I easily take.
My parent and I produce one another,
The mother the daughter, the daughter the mother.

*"All that we caught, we left behind and
carried away all that we did not catch."*

*This riddle, recorded by Plutarch, caused the death of
Homer, through vexation at his inability to solve it. It
was propounded by some boys whom Homer met as
they were returning from fishing, when he asked them
if they had caught anything.*
    (They referred to fleas or flies, not to fish.)

MOUNTAIN SEPTEMBER

Purple firewood . . . drooping
In the heat of noonday sun;
Down the white trail's careless looping
Little vagrant dust puffs run . . .
Where the tamaracks are sighing
Knotted branches drop their showers . . .
Yellow gold . . . The summer . . . dying
Through the lazy gold-shot hours.

PRAIRIE SEPTEMBER

Grass—burned sere with wind and sun;
Waterholes and streambeds—choked with mud;
Bawling steers—ribby, weak and hungry;
Bannered smoke from prairie fires
In my throat.

"I Have Known Green Mountain Meadows"

Yes, I have known green mountain meadows,
And swamps where blackbirds call,
And pools where stones and water glisten
In the bright hot rays of noontime sun;
And I have travelled newer, longer trails,
Feeling the tug of packstraps on my back,
Hearing the soft slow tread of mountain men—
(My ancestors who knew the Oberland)
Re-echoed on Montana's scarce-known hills.
And I have camped at night by ice-walled lakes
Above the clouds . . .

I wonder why the pavements hurt my feet.

All by JOHN C. FROHLICHER

December 24

St. Gregory of Spoleto, martyr, 304. Saints Thrasilla and Emiliana, virgins.

For a picture of Christmas Eve, in the olden time, we can desire none more graphic than that furnished by Sir Walter Scott in *Marmion*.

> 'On Christmas Eve the bells were rung;
> On Christmas Eve the mass was sung;
> That only night, in all the year,
> Saw the stoled priest the chalice rear.
> The damsel donned her kirtle sheen;
> The hall was dressed with holly green;
> Forth to the wood did merry-men go,
> To gather in the mistletoe.
> Then opened wide the baron's hall
> To vassal, tenant, serf, and all;
> Power laid his rod of rule aside,
> And Ceremony doffed his pride.
> The heir, with roses in his shoes,
> That night might village partner choose.
> The lord, underogating, share
> The vulgar game of 'post and pair.'
> All hailed, with uncontrolled delight,
> And general voice, the happy night,
> That to the cottage, as the crown,
> Brought tidings of salvation down!

I with borrowed silver shine,
What you see is none of mine.
First I show you but a quarter,
Like the bow that guards the Tartar:
Then the half, and then the whole,
Ever dancing round the pole.

—SWIFT, *On the Moon*

By the light of the moon, my friend, Pierrot,
Lend me thy pen to write a word,
My candle is out, I've no more fire,
Open your door to me for the love of God.

—FRENCH *folk song*

The man in the moon
Who sails through the sky
   Is a most courageous skipper;
Yet he made a mistake
When he tried to take
   A drink of milk from the Dipper.
He dipped it into the "Milky Way,"
   And slowly, cautiously filled it;
But the Great Bear growled,
And the Little Bear Howled
   And scared him so that he spilled it.

—"ST. NICHOLAS"

He slept beneath the Moon,
  He basked beneath the Sun;
He lived a life of going-to-do,
  And died with nothing done.
     *—Epitaph—*JAMES ALBERY

Everyone is a moon and has a dark side
which he never shows to anybody.

—MARK TWAIN, *Pudd'nhead Wilson*

A FAREWELL

My fairest child, I have no song to give you;
   No lark could pipe to skies so dull and gray;
Yet, ere we part, one lesson I can leave you
   For every day.

Be good, sweet maid, and let who will be clever;
   Do noble things, not dream them, all day long:
And so make life, death, and that vast forever
   One grand, sweet song.

—CHARLES KINGSLEY.

THE RAVEN

Once upon a midnight dreary, while I pondered,
   weak and weary,
Over many a quaint and curious volume of forgotten
   lore,
While I nodded, nearly napping, suddenly there came
   a tapping,
As of some one gently rapping, rapping at my
   chamber door.
" 'Tis some visitor," I muttered, "tapping at my
   chamber door —
   Only this, and nothing more."

—EDGAR ALLAN POE

Light is above us, and color around us; but if we have not light and color in our eyes, we shall not perceive them outside us.
   — GOETHE

FINISH
by
CARL SANDBURG
from Smoke and Steel

Death comes once, let it be easy.
Ring one bell for me once, let it go at that.
Or ring no bell at all, better yet.

Sing one song if I die.
Sing John Brown's Body or Shout All Over
    God's Heaven.
Or sing nothing at all, better yet.

Death comes once, let it be easy.

DEATH SNIPS PROUD MEN
by
CARL SANDBURG
from Smoke and Steel

Death is stronger than all the governments because the
  governments are men and men die and then death
  laughs: Now you see 'em, now you don't.

Death is stronger than all proud men and so death snips
  proud men on the nose, throws a pair of dice and says:
  Read 'em and weep.

Death sends a radiogram every day: When I want you I'll
  drop in—and then one day he comes with a master-key
  and lets himself in and says: We'll go now.

Death is a nurse mother with big arms: 'Twon't hurt you
  at all; it's your time now; you just need a long sleep,
  child; what have you had anyhow better than sleep?

MUTABILITY

by PERCY B. SHELLEY

Published by Mrs. Shelley, Posthumous Poems, 1824

I

The flower that smiles to-day
To-morrow dies;
All that we wish to stay,
Tempts and then flies.
What is this world's delight?
Lightning that mocks the night,
Brief even as bright.

II

Virtue, how frail it is!
Friendship how rare!
Love, how it sells poor bliss
For proud despair!
But we, though soon they fall,
Survive their joy and all
Which ours we call.

III

Whilst skies are blue and bright,
Whilst flowers are gay,
Whilst eyes that change ere night
Make glad the day,
Whilst yet the calm hours creep,
Dream thou — and from thy sleep
Then wake to weep.

Heaven knows we need never be ashamed of our tears for they are rain upon the blinding dust of earth, overlying our hard hearts.
— CHARLES DICKENS — Great Expectations

A CHILD OF TWELVE

A child most infantine
Yet wandering far beyond that innocent age
In all but its sweet looks and mien divine.

.   .   .   .

She moved upon this earth a shape of brightness,
A power, that from its objects scarcely drew
One impulse of her being — in her lightness
Most like some radiant cloud of morning dew,
Which wanders through the waste air's pathless
    blue,
To nourish some far desert; she did seem
Beside me, gathering beauty as she grew,
Like the bright shade of some immortal dream
Which walks, when tempest sleeps, the wave of
    life's dark stream.
As mine own shadow was this child to me.

.   .   .   .

This playmate sweet,
This child of twelve years old.

— PERCY BYSSHE SHELLEY
"The Revolt of Islam"

Sing me a song of a lad that is gone;
Say, could that lad be I?
Merry of soul he sailed on a day
Over the sea to Skye.

—R. L. STEVENSON, *A Lad That is Gone*

PROVERBS FOR APRIL

"If it thunders on All Fool's Day,
It brings good crops of corn and hay."

"A cold April
The barn will fill."

An April flood
Carries away the frog and his brood."

If the oak precede the ash,
We shall have both rain and splash;
If the ash precede the oak,
We shall have both fire and smoke;
But if they both come out together,
We shall then have lovely weather.

OLD RHYME

*Be very vigilant over thy child in the April of his under-
standing, lest the frosts of May nip his blossoms.*

— FRANCIS QUARLES

PROVERBS FOR MAY

*"Change not a clout
Till May be out."*

*"A swarm of bees in May
Is worth a load of hay."*

*"Mist in May and heat in June
Make the harvest right soon."*

*"May, full of cold and rain,
Much straw and little grain."*

"A cold May brings no riches."

"A hot May makes a fat churchyard."

The Face on the Barroom Floor

This classic, by Hugh D'Arcy, was first printed in 1887, and titled *The Face Upon the Floor*. It is amusing to note that it was never intended to point out the perils of strong drink, but merely to portray the degradation of an artist tortured by the loss of his sweetheart. The poem was seized by the W. C. T. U., and later the Anti-Saloon League, the title altered, and millions of copies distributed as propaganda.

"If I thought my poem had done anything to help Prohibition," said D'Arcy, in 1925, "I would go take a running jump into the Hudson."

Too long to quote in full, the poem follows the familiar "my-pal-stole-my-gal" theme. The artist, "gone gutter," drifts into a barroom, begging a drink. Fortified by a swig of whiskey, he tells his tale in too-many verses. Here are the concluding stanzas—which will doubtless prove ample for our purpose:

"Say, boys, if you give me another whiskey I'll be glad,
And I'll draw right here a picture of the face that drove me
    mad.
Give me that piece of chalk with which you mark the baseball
    score—
You shall see the lovely Madeline upon the barroom floor."
Another drink, and with chalk in hand, the vagabond began
To sketch a face that well might buy the soul of any man.
Then as he placed another lock upon the stately head,
With a fearful shriek, he leaped and fell across the picture—
    dead.

How far can you see at night!

Cross examining a man who had witnessed an accident:
Did you see the man on the train?
Yes, sir.
Where was he?
About thirty cars back from the engine.
Where were you?
I was back of the tender of the engine.
About what time of night was it?
Eleven o'clock.
Do you mean to tell me that you saw that man thirty cars
   away at eleven o'clock at night?
Yes, sir.
How far do you think you can see at night?
'Bout a million miles, I reckon—how far is it to the moon?

BIRTHSTONES
For laundresses, the soapstone.
For architects, the cornerstone.
For cooks, the puddingstone.
For soldiers, the bloodstone.
For politicians, the blarneystone.
For borrowers, the touchstone.
For policemen, the pavingstone.
For stock brokers, the curbstone.
For burglars, the keystone.
For tourists, the Yellowstone.
For beauties, the peachstone.
For editors, the grindstone.
For motorists, the milestone.
For pedestrians, the tombstone.

Say it with flowers,
Say it with sweets,
Say it with kisses,
Say it with eats,
Say it with jewelry,
Say it with drink,
But always be careful
Not to say it with ink.

FROM THE SICK STOCK RIDER

by ADAM LINDSAY GORDON

In these hours when life is ebbing, how those days when
    life was young
    Come back to us; how clearly I recall
Even the yarns Jack Hall invented, and the songs Jem
    Roper sung!
    And where are now Jem Roper and Jack Hall?

Aye! nearly all our comrades of the old colonial school,
    Our ancient boon companions, Ned, are gone;
Hard livers for the most part, somewhat reckless as a rule,
    It seems that you and I are left alone.

There was Hughes, who got in trouble through that busi-
    ness with the cards,
    It matters little what become of him;
But a steer ripp'd up MacPherson in the Cooraminta
    yards,
    And Sullivan was drown'd at Sink-or-swim;

And Mostyn – poor Frank Mostyn – died at last a fearful
    wreck,
    In "the horrors," at the Upper Wandinong,
And Carisbrooke, the rider, at the Horsefall broke his
    neck,
    Faith! the wonder was he saved his neck so long!

Ah! those days and nights we squandered at the Logans'
    in the glen –
    The Logans, man and wife, have long been dead.
Elsie's tallest girl seems taller than your little Elsie then;
    And Ethel is a woman grown and wed.

I've had my share of pastime, and I've done my share of
    toil,
    And life is short – the longest life a span;
I care not now to tarry for the corn or for the oil,
    Or for the wine that maketh glad the heart of man.
For good undone and gifts misspent and resolutions vain,
    'Tis somewhat late to trouble. This I know –
I should live the same life over, if I had to live again;
    And the chances are I go where most men go.

THE LONG-DISTANCE RUNNER

CHARMUS ran a three-miles race,
    Ran with five competitors.
He obtained the seventh place:
    But how could he get it, as
Only six men ran? Now, note
    That a certain friend of his,
Running in his overcoat,
    Cheered him onward, and that is
Why, as I have said before,
    Charmus only came in seventh.
Had there been but four friends more,
    He'd have surely been eleventh.

— NICARCHUS

AHEAD OF A POSSE
by
JOHN C. FROHLICHER

A half-spent hoss and an empty gun;
An arm where the bright blood spills;
He's tryin' to join the wild bunch—
The wild bunch in the hills.

He's run his brand on the wrong man's cow,
So he's riding the outlaw trail
With grim-faced men behind him now,
An' they'll not take him to jail!

For blotting brands, in the old wild west
Judge Lynch presents the bills,
So he's tryin' to join the wild bunch—
The wild bunch in the hills.

WHEN I HEARD THE LEARN'D ASTRONOMER
by
WALT WHITMAN, *Leaves of Grass*

When I heard the learn'd astronomer;
When the proofs, the figures, were ranged in columns
    before me;
When I was shown the charts and the diagrams, to add,
    divide, and measure them;
When I, sitting, heard the astronomer, where he lectured
    with much applause in the lecture-room,
How soon, unaccountable, I became tired and sick;
Till rising and gliding out, I wander'd off by myself,
In the mystical moist night-air, and from time to time,
Look'd up in perfect silence at the stars.

OTHERS MAY PRAISE WHAT THEY LIKE
First published in "Drum-Taps," by WALT WHITMAN

Others may praise what they like;
But I, from the banks of the running Missouri, praise
    nothing, in art, or aught else,
Till it has well inhaled the atmosphere of this river — also
    the western prairie-scent,
And fully exudes it again.

GREAT ARE THE MYTHS
by WALT WHITMAN

Great is To-day, and beautiful,
It is good to live in this age — there never was any better.

Great are the plunges, throes, triumphs, downfalls of
    Democracy,
Great the reformers, with their lapses and screams,
Great the daring and venture of sailors, on new
    explorations.

Great are Yourself and Myself,
We are just as good and bad as the oldest and youngest or
    any,
What the best and worst did, we could do,
What they felt, do not we feel it in ourselves?
What they wished, do we not wish the same?"

THE ROAD'S LAST TURN

Let me but live my life from year to year,
With forward face and unreluctant soul,
Not hastening to, nor turning from the goal;
Nor mourning things that disappear
In the dim past, nor holding back in fear
From what the future veils; but with a whole
And happy heart, that pays its toll
To youth and age, and travels on with cheer.
So let the way wind up the hill or down,
Through rough or smooth, the journey will be joy,
Still seeking what I sought when but a boy—
New friendship, high adventure, and a crown,
I shall grow old, but never lose life's zest,
Because the road's last turn will be the best.

Henry van Dyke.

Courtesy of Chicago's American

MR. PRESIDENT:
"You'll certainly have to do better than this"—

by WENDELL SMITH

—Jungle Jim Rivera, the most unlikely candidate to receive a "pass" from the President of the United States, suddenly turned his back on the crowd of players lined up along the first base line and drifted in the direction of the "end zone," running as fast as possible.

President Kennedy, having shed his top coat, let fly with the ball that signified the opening of the new baseball season.

Jungle Jim, clearly in the open, gathered in the toss as gracefully and dramatically as possible, danced a hilarious jig, and then raced to the Presidential box in quest of an autograph. When he reached his destination, Mickey Vernon, manager of the Washington Senators, reached for the historic ball and said:

"Give it to me, I'll get you the autograph."

Rivera, who apparently trusts the Senators' pilot implicitly, did as ordered. The President accepted the ball from Vernon, signed it, and asked, innocently:

"Who is he?"

Vernon identified Rivera, saying:

"Jim Rivera, an outfielder for the White Sox."

The President, surrounded by cabinet members, including Vice President Johnson, recalled:

"O, yes, I remember reading about him."

He handed the ball back to Vernon, who in turn gave it to Rivera.

Jungle Jim examined the prize carefully, noted that

the President's signature was hardly legible in comparison with the Vice President's, and shook his head. Looking up at the world's most influential personality, Rivera said:

"*What's this? This is just a scribble on the ball. I can hardly make it out.*"

Then the personable outfielder, hardly a diplomat, said to the President:

"*You'll certainly have to do better than this, John.*"

Kennedy looked at Rivera with a surprised expression, laughed, and sat down. He is not accustomed to such informality. Rivera walked away, clutching the ball and grinning.

Neither Kennedy, nor the government dignitaries who accompanied him to the baseball inaugural will be on hand Wednesday night when the Sox and Washington resume their warfare here.

But they'll long remember the brash, yet pleasant Rivera as the only player who ever dared call a President by his first name.

Perhaps it was a desire to see Jungle Jim in action that kept the Chief Executive in his seat thru the entire nine innings.

EPIGRAM

(From Westminister Drollery. 1671.)

A WATCH lost in a tavern! That's a Crime;
Then see how men by drinking lose their time.

The Watch kept Time; and if Time will away,
I see no reason why the Watch should stay.

You say the Key hung out, and you forgot to lock it,
Time will not be kept pris'ner in a Pocket.

Henceforth, if you will keep your Watch, this do,
Pocket your Watch, and watch your Pocket, too.

Barbara Frietchie

by JOHN GREENLEAF WHITTIER

Up from the meadows rich with corn,
Clear in the cool September morn,

The clustered spires of Frederick stand
Green-walled by the hills of Maryland.

Round about them orchards sweep,
Apple and peach tree fruited deep,

Fair as a garden of the Lord,
To the eyes of the famished rebel horde,

On that pleasant morn of the early fall
When Lee marched over the mountain wall,—

Over the mountains, winding down,
Horse and foot into Frederick town.

Forty flags with their silver stars,
Forty flags with their crimson bars,

Flapped in the morning wind; the sun
Of noon looked down, and saw not one.

Up rose old Barbara Frietchie then,
Bowed with her fourscore years and ten;

Bravest of all in Frederick town,
She took up the flag the men hauled down;

In her attic-window the staff she set,
To show that one heart was loyal yet.

Up the street came the rebel tread,
Stonewall Jackson riding ahead.

Under his slouch hat left and right
He glanced: the old flag met his sight.

"Halt!"—the dust-brown ranks stood fast;
"Fire!"—out blazed the rifle-blast.

It shivered the window, pane and sash;
It rent the banner with seam and gash.

Quick, as it fell, from the broken staff
Dame Barbara snatched the silken scarf;

She leaned far out on the window-sill,
And shook it forth with a royal will.

"Shot, if you must, this old gray head,
But spare your country's flag," she said.

A shade of sadness, a blush of shame,
Over the face of the leader came;

The nobler nature within him stirred
To life at that woman's deed and word:

"Who touches a hair of yon gray head
Dies like a dog! March on!" he said.

All day long through Frederick street
Sounded the tread of marching feet;

All day long that free flag tost
Over the heads of the rebel host.

Ever its torn folds rose and fell
On the loyal winds that loved it well;

And through the hill-gaps sunset light
Shone over it with a warm good-night.

Barbara Frietchie's work is o'er,
And the rebel rides on his raids no more.

Honor to her! and let a tear
Fall, for her sake, on Stonewall's bier.

Over Barbara Frietchie's grave,
Flag of freedom and union wave!

Peace and order and beauty draw
Round thy symbol of light and law;

And ever the stars above look down
On thy stars below in Frederick town.

JOHN GREENLEAF WHITTIER.

"My right has been rolled up;
my left has been driven back;
my center has been smashed. I
have ordered an advance from
all directions."

— MARSHAL FOCH

RATING WORDS BY THEIR IMPORTANCE

The FIVE most important words, *I am proud of you.*
The FOUR most important words, *What is your opinion?*
The THREE most important words, *If you please.*
The TWO most important words, *Thank you.*
The One most important word, *I.*

Petition For A Life of Contentment

Lord make me a channel of Thy peace.
That where there is hatred—I may
    bring love,
That where there is wrong—I may
    bring the spirit of forgiveness
That where there is discord—I may
    bring harmony,
That where there is error—I may bring
    truth.
That where there is doubt—I may bring
    faith,
That where there is despair—I may
    bring hope,
That where there are shadows—I may
    bring Thy light,
That where there is sadness—I may
    bring joy.

Lord, grant that I may seek rather
To comfort—than to be comforted;
To understand—than to be understood;
To love—than to be loved;

For
It is by giving—that one receives;
It is by self-forgetting—that one finds;
It is by forgiving—that one is forgiven;
It is by dying—that one awakens
    to eternal life.

ST. FRANCIS OF ASSISI

Be True Thyself

Thou must be true thyself,
  If thou the truth wouldst teach;
Thy soul must overflow, if thou
  Another's soul wouldst reach!
It needs the overflow of heart
  To give the lips full speech.

Think truly, and thy thoughts
  Shall the world's famine feed;
Speak truly, and each word of thine
  Shall be a fruitful seed;
Live truly, and thy life shall be
  A great and noble creed.

HORATIO BONAR.

The Shepherd Boy Sings in the Valley of Humiliation

He that is down needs fear no fall,
  He that is low, no pride;
He that is humble ever shall
  Have God to be his guide.

I am content with what I have,
  Little be it or much:
And, Lord, contentment still I crave,
  Because Thou savest such.

Fullness to such a burden is
  That go on pilgrimage:
Here little, and hereafter bliss,
  Is best from age to age.

JOHN BUNYAN.

"Mother Earth Who Never Failed Was Keeping Her Faith Again"

There it was the Wheat, the Wheat! The little seed, long planted, germinating in the deep, dark furrows of the soil, straining, swelling, suddenly in one night had burst upward to the light. The wheat had come up. It was before him, around him, everywhere, illimitable, immeasurable. The winter brownness of the ground was overlaid with a little shimmer of green. The promise of the sowing was being fulfilled. The earth, the loyal mother, who never failed, who never disappointed, was keeping her faith again.

—FRANK NORRIS
Epic of the Wheat

The idea of what is true merit should also be often presented to youth, explained and impressed on their minds as consisting in an inclination, joined with an ability, to serve mankind, over country, friends and family, which ability is (with the blessing of God) to be acquired or greatly increased by true learning; and should be the great aim and end of all learning.

—BEN FRANKLIN
Proposals

At every age one may fight
and triumph, but one must be
young, and not have experienced
the inevitable caprices of fortune,
the sly betrayals of battle, in
order to throw oneself without
reserve into the fray, with the
careless frivolity of youth!

—JURIEN DE LAGRAVIERE
Vice Admiral of France

It is strange, but nevertheless true, that mankind frequently ignores even the common courtesies and the rights of those who are without power or influence, in business or society. On the contrary, he approaches with humility, courtesy, and caution those, he, perhaps in his heart despises, if they are in exalted stations of power or wealth. And we find, also, that he is able to control his passions most amazingly when in the presence of his superiors, or when it is to his interest so to do. Yet those same passions seem to be above his management or control when he is with those who are beneath him, and unable outwardly to resent his affronts.

—JAMES NORTHCOTE

Words are arrows and should not be shot at random. Silence is a gift without peril, and a treasure without enemies. Those who speak are not serious enough, and those that hear are too serious.

There is a natural dignity in great minds, which makes them pass by, with a total disregard, the snarl of envy, or the clamors of malice.

The energy and versatility of the mind depend upon action no less than the vigor and agility of the body.

Do not stand idly waiting
For some greater work to do,
Fortune is a lazy goddess,
She will never come to you.
Go and toil in any vineyard
Do not fear to do or dare,
If you want a field of labor,
You can find it anywhere.

All beyond enough is too much

The wants of nature are few. It is the function of reason to regulate both the taste and the appetite; and those who are governed by her laws, will be enabled to leave their wealth, their health, and their example as rich endowments to their heirs.

All beyond enough is too much, all beyond nourishment is luxury, all beyond decency is extravagance. Intemperance has a smiling and alluring aspect, but a dreadful retinue, consisting of a whole assemblage of diseases, for death has been its cook and has infused a slow poison into every sauce.

Extraordinary luxury is to property what a plague is to health. It is equally contagious and equally destructive. It is the disease of which not only individuals, but the noblest monarchies, and the most flourishing states have died.

The pleasure of adulation, however false, goes so far, that the greatest of our enemies makes himself agreeable, when he imposes upon us with it; and the best of our friends seldom care to set us straight. Few men are so wise as to prefer useful reproofs to treacherous praise. Therefore, flattery will never be out of style, so long as there are those to give it, and fools to take it. There is nothing that a man will not believe in his own favor.

—JUVENAL

The seven mottos of the seven sages of ancient Greece:

1. Know thyself.
2. Consider the end.
3. Who hateth suretyship is sure.
4. Most men are bad.
5. Avoid extremes.
6. Seize time by the forelock.
7. Nothing is impossible to industry.

...*the finest things in life*

The finest things in life are those
　　You neither sell nor buy,
A bursting bud — a bird that sings,
　　A glowing Western sky;
And friends to love, these are, indeed,
　　Well worth their weight in gold,
And may you know the joys which
　　You will forever behold.
　　　　　— CAROLINE BOWES TOMBO.

MAKING FRIENDS

Making friends is a lot of fun
Shaking hands with everyone
Hearing what each has to say
As we meet them day by day
Swapping smiles and trading cheer
Makes us happy while we're here
'Cause all the joy of life depends
Just on the art of making and keeping friends

I mistrust the judgment of every man in a case in which his own wishes are concerned.
　　　　　— DUKE OF WELLINGTON

A CONGRESSMAN'S LAMENT

Among life's dying embers,
These are my regrets!
When I'm right no one remembers,
When I'm wrong no one forgets.

On Sir Isaac Newton

The Earth was but a platform for thy power,
Whereon to watch and work, by day and night;
The Moon to thee was but heaven's evening flower;
The Sun a loftier argument of light;
Each Planet was thy fellow traveler bright,
In vision,— and, in thought, still nearer home:
Throughout the Universe thy soul took flight,
And touch'd at suns whose rays may never come.
Though star-tranced Tycho and the thought sublime
Of Kepler fathom'd Heaven's infinity,
To thee 'twas left to prove the laws that chime
Through spheres and atoms,— being, and to be:
Profound alike in thy humility,—
"A child that gather'd shells, kneeling beside the sea."

If this little world to-night
    Suddenly should fall through space
In a hissing, headlong flight,
    Shrivelling from off its face,
As it falls into the sun,
    In an instant every trace
Of the little crawling things —
    Ants, philosophers, and lice,
Cattle, cockroaches, and kings,
    Beggars, millionaires, and mice,
Men and maggots,— all as one
    As it falls into the sun,—
Who can say but at the same
    Instant from some planet far
A child may watch us and exclaim:
    "See the pretty shooting star!"

— OLIVER HERFORD

TO THE GENTLE READER

"A French writer (whom I love well) speaks of three
kinds of companions — men, women, and books."
                                        —SIR JOHN DAVYS

Three kinds of companions, men, women and books,
    Were enough, said the elderly Sage, for his ends.
And the women we deem that he chose for their looks,
    And the men for their cellars: the books were his friends;
"Man delights me not," often, "nor woman," but books
Are the best of good comrades in loneliest nooks.

For man will be wrangling — for women will fret
    About everything infinitesimal small:
Like the Sage in our Plato, I'm "anxious to get
    On the side" — on the sunnier side — "of a wall."
Let the wind of the world toss the nations like rooks,
If only you'll leave me at peace with my Books.
                                        —ANDREW LANG

            I have lived and I have loved;
            I have waked and I have slept;
            I have sung and I have danced;
            I have smiled and I have wept;
            I have won and wasted treasure;
            I have had my fill of pleasure;
            And all these things were weariness,
            And some of them were dreariness,
            And all these things — but two things
            Were emptiness and pain:
            And Love — it was the best of them;
            And Sleep — worth all the rest of them.

    Reading ends in melancholy!
        Wine breeds vices and diseases!
    Wealth's but a care, and Love but folly;
        Only Friendship truly pleases!
    My wealth, my books, my flask, my MOLLY,
        Farewell all, if Friendship ceases!
                                        —MATTHEW PRIOR

SIR, I WOULD RATHER BE RIGHT THAN BE PRESIDENT.

By Henry Clay

[An American statesman and orator; born in Virginia, April 12, 1777; elected United States senator from Kentucky, 1806; to the House of Representatives, 1811, and chosen speaker; commissioner to sign the treaty of peace with England, 1814; a candidate for the Presidency, 1824 and 1844; senator, 1831; resigned, 1842; reelected, 1848, and served until his death, June 29, 1852.]

A remark which became proverbial; made to Mr. Preston of Kentucky, who told him that the compromise measures of 1850, which he advocated as a means of preserving the Union, would injure his chances for the presidency by alienating the Northern, or anti-slavery, Whigs. Clay's motto then and always was, "I know no North, no South, no East, no West"; which he first used when taunted by a Southern senator with being unfaithful to his section. During the debate in the Senate on the compromise measures, he declared, "If Kentucky should to-morrow unfurl the banner of resistance unjustly, I will never fight under that banner. I owe a paramount allegiance to the whole Union,— a subordinate one to my own State." And again he said, "The senator speaks of Virginia being my country. The Union, sir, is my country." Patrick Henry said in the Continental Congress, Sept. 5, 1774, "I am not a Virginian, but an American," and Daniel Webster declared, "I was born an American, I live an American, I shall die an American."

Two things indicate weakness,— to be silent when it is proper to speak, and to speak when it is proper to be silent.

—Persian Proverb

GIVE ME

Leave to enjoy myself. That place, that does
Contain my books, the best companions, is
To me a glorious court, where hourly I
Converse with the old sages and philosophers.
And sometimes for variety, I confer
With kings and emperors, and weigh their counsels;
Calling their victories, if unjustly got,
Unto a strict account; and, in my fancy,
Deface their ill-planned statues. Can I then
Part with such constant pleasures, to embrace
Uncertain vanities? No; be it your care
To augment a heap of wealth; it shall be mine
To increase in knowledge. Lights there, for my study!

—JOHN FLETCHER, *The Elder Brother*

FRIENDS

You ask me "why I like him." Nay,
I cannot; nay, I would not, say.
I think it vile to pigeonhole
The pros and cons of a kindred soul.

You "wonder he should be my friend."
But then why should you comprehend?
Thank God for this — a new — surprise:
My eyes, remember, are not your eyes.

Cherish this one small mystery;
And marvel not that love can be
"In Spite of all his many flaws."
In spite? Supposing I said "Because."

A truce, a truce to questioning:
"We two are friends" tells everything.
Yet if you *must* know, this is why:
Because he is he and I am I.

—E. V. LUCAS

WHEN WE WERE POOR

"I wish the good old times would come again," she said, "when we were not quite so rich. I do not mean, that I want to be poor; but there was a middle state" – so she was pleased to ramble on – "in which I am sure we were a great deal happier. A purchase is but a purchase, now that you have money enough and to spare. Formerly it used to be a triumph. When we coveted a cheap luxury (and O! how much ado I had to get you to consent in those times!) – we were used to having a debate two or three days before, and to weigh the *for* and *against*, and think what we might spare it out of, and what saving we could hit upon, that should be an equivalent. A thing was worth buying then, when we felt the money that we paid for it . . . When you came home with twenty apologies for laying out a less number of shillings upon that print after Lionardo, which we christened the 'Lady Blanche'; when you looked at the purchase, and thought of the money – and thought of the money, and loked again at that picture – was there is no pleasure in being a poor man? Now you have nothing to do but to walk into Colnaghi's and buy a wilderness of Lionardos. Yet do you?"

–CHARLES LAMB

Go plant the bean when the moon is light,
And you will find that this is right;
Plant the potatoes when the moon is dark,
And to this line you always hark;
But if you vary from this rule,
You will find you are a fool;
If you always follow this rule to the end
You will always have money to spend.

PERSISTENCE

NOTHING in the world can take the place
of persistence,
    Talent will not;
Nothing is more common than unsuccessful
men with talent.
    Genius will not;
Unrewarded genius is almost a proverb.
    Education will not;
The world is full of educated derelicts.
Persistence and determination alone are
    omnipotent.
The slogan
            "Press On"
                      has solved
and always will solve the problems of the
    human race.

                         —ANONYMOUS

There is a tide in the affairs of men
which, taken at the flood, leads on to fortune;
omitted, all the voyage of their life
Is bound in shallows and in miseries.

                       —SHAKESPEARE

There are some men who are Fortune's
favorites, and who like cats, light
forever on their legs.

                       —COLTON

When a true genius appears in the world, you may know
him by this sign—that the dunces are all in a Confederacy
against him.

                       —SWIFT

WHY I'M A JUNGLE MEDIC

By THOMAS A. DOOLEY, M.D.

By courtesy of IBM magazine *THINK*.

In the jungles of Laos, near the China border, Dr. Dooley was dispensing his own kind of foreign aid—medicine mixed with compassion. Here is his story of the results.

MOST intelligent and mature Americans know the duties of their citizenship. Those of us burdened with being over-privileged know we must help those burdened with being under-privileged. We manifest this awareness through help —private, corporate and national. Let me tell you of one small effort. Let me paint a picture for you. Come to my tiny hut-of-a-hospital in the village of Nam Tha, northern-most village of Laos. Nam Tha is perched precariously on the rim of the red hell of Communist China. Laos is the fingerlike projection of still-free Southeast Asia that pokes into the underbelly of China. Nam Tha is not just another Asian village. It is unique because in it you will find St. Patrick's Hospital, run by my five young American corps-men and myself. Here we are trying to light our candle rather than curse the darkness of the decade. Here we are trying to invest some of our humanity in the great struggle of the time.

To get to Nam Tha is not easy. First the reader must fly half a world away, to Bangkok. From New York it takes 44 hours, with a short stop in Paris, Rome, Athens, Cairo, Cal-cutta and Rangoon. At the swank international terminal in Bangkok you can pause to eat a fine steak and change from a clipper ship to a DC-3. Two hours straight north towards China will bring you to the muddy airport of Vientiane, capital of Loas, the Kingdom of a Million Elephants.

In Vientiane you are plunged back through the rivers of time, perhaps a century or two. On the main streets, only a few of which are paved, you will find the rickshaw and the bicycle-driven rickshaw, battling with antiquated taxis, buffalo carts and an occasional elephant. This vehicular

The essence of good citizenship is unselfishness and a determi-nation to make the world a better and happier place without thought of personal gain.

constipation is called "traffic". . . Within an hour or so you may locate the boat dock, where, with some struggle, you can rent several pirogues. These are long canoes made by splitting a log and digging out the center section. A flying platform is attached fore and aft. Here the natives squat and steer with long oars. A few more natives sit along the sides of these 20-foot canoes and paddle. You are going up river, so there will be plenty of paddling. Down river you can ride the rapids.

You might be growing impatient to get to the 15th century; after all it has been about three days since you left Manhattan's towers to come to Asia. Americans are an impatient lot. But no one in Laos is in a rush. Perhaps the 110-degree heat has something to do with it. Perhaps the humidity. Perhaps the fact that nearly everyone in the country has intestinal parasites, many have malaria, and a high number hack out their lives with tuberculosis. Anyway, let's go slow, be careful. On both sides of this Mekong River are myriads of dirty little villages. Many abound with Communist bandits.

As you have told the boatman you are going to the north to see the white witch doctor named Dooley, you will get first-class care. Your oarsmen will probably weave a large palm leaf covering to provide a curved roof over your head, as you sit, hunched over, on the wet floor of the canoe.

Now you are ready to shove off . . . and paddle back through the centuries. No rush. The trip from Vientiane to my village of Nam Tha will take you quite some time—about eight days.

The geography is magnificent. On the sides of the river the jungle is so thick that there hardly seems to be a space to put a finger through. There is an extravagant monotony of unceasing green. You will be dazzled by the occasional

What is a communist? One who has yearnings for equal division of unequal earnings.

— EPIGRAM, EBENEZER ELLIOT

luxuriant scarlet splash of the frangipani tree. Under a blazing sun you row up river at a crawling pace. There will be areas where it seems that the heaviness of the climate will make you suffocate. In other places, your spirit will be lifted by the watchful, enormous trees that soar up to the sky like cathedral pillars.

Your head will swim with the dizziness of it all. Along the tree limbs you will see the clinging, tenacious tendrils and trailers, the parasites which claw into the fleshy bark and try to consume the tree. But the delicate, leafed canopy against God's sky will flower and bloom, and the wild monkey and jay will dart back and forth, angry that you have disturbed them. You will see birds so blue as to enchant the heart of Maeterlinck.

Night falls unpremeditated. No long, drawn-out parting of the semi-worlds of light and dark, dawn or dusk. The sun sets in a tangle of colors, and with a rioting of clouds the black night of Asia suddenly opens and engulfs the jungle life. Immense night has come. Often the stars and the moon will not rise. Nothingness.

This kingdom of Laos is one of the most backward, undeveloped, primitive areas of the world; yet the people— many of whom are dying in their own decay—possess a culture and a gentleness antedating the Western World. The ancestors of those villagers who are staring out at you from the river's edges are the people who designed and built the glories of Ankor Wat, the pagodas, stupas and temples of upper Thailand and Burma. These are a fine and gracious people. But these are a people forgotten by Western civilization. As we clawed and grasped for progress upward on the rungs of technology, these people were left behind. To them we owe something. We have a oneness with all men.

Progress is the law of life, man is not man as yet.
— PARACELSUS V, ROBERT BROWNING

Learn to die, thou that
  readest these words engraved
  upon my tomb,
And deeply impress upon
  thy heart my last words;
Thy only safety is to serve God;
  All else is vanity.

Do therefore now what thou
  wouldst wish to have done
  when about to die.
Eternity depends upon a
  moment; the tree
  lies where it falls;
Therefore, I pray you, learn
  to die, learn to die!

—Epitaph composed by
ALEXANDER VII

———

To suffer woes which Hope thinks infinite;
To forgive wrongs darker than death or night;
  To defy power, which seems omnipotent;
To love, and bear! to hope till Hope creates
From its own wreck the thing it contemplates!
  Neither to change, nor falter, nor repent!
This, like thy glory, Titan, is to be
Good, great and joyous, beautiful and free;
This is along Life, Joy, Empire, and Victory.

— P. B. SHELLEY—*The Ideal*